WHAT ARE THE BOOKS OF 1–2 TIMOTHY & TITUS?

Kids' Guides to God's Word Series

What Is the Book of Genesis?
What Is the Book of Exodus?
What Is the Book of Leviticus?
What Is the Book of Numbers?
What Is the Book of Deuteronomy?
What Is the Book of Joshua?
What Is the Book of Judges?
What Is the Book of Ruth?
What Is the Book of 1 Samuel?
What Is the Book of 2 Samuel?
What Is the Book of 1 Kings?
What Is the Book of 2 Kings?
What Are the Books of 1–2 Chronicles?
What Are the Books of Ezra & Nehemiah?
What Is the Book of Esther?
What Is the Book of Job?
What Is the Book of Psalms?
What Is the Book of Proverbs?
What Is the Book of Ecclesiastes?
What Are the Books of Song of Songs & Lamentations?
What Is the Book of Isaiah?
What Is the Book of Jeremiah?
What Is the Book of Ezekiel?
What Is the Book of Daniel?
What Are the Books of Hosea–Micah?
What Are the Books of Nahum–Malachi?

What Is the Gospel of Matthew?
What Is the Gospel of Mark?
What Is the Gospel of Luke?
What Is the Gospel of John?
What Is the Book of Acts?
What Is the Book of Romans?
What Is the Book of 1 Corinthians?
What Is the Book of 2 Corinthians?
What Is the Book of Galatians?
What Is the Book of Ephesians?
What Is the Book of Philippians?
What Are the Books of Colossians & Philemon?
What Are the Books of 1–2 Thessalonians?
What Are the Books of 1–2 Timothy & Titus?
What Is the Book of Hebrews?
What Is the Book of James?
What Are the Books of 1–2 Peter & Jude?
What Are the Books of 1-3 John?
What Is the Book of Revelation?

What Are the Books of

1-2 TIMOTHY & TITUS?

Michael Whitworth

ISBN 978-1-971767-34-5

Published by Start2Finish
Bend, Oregon 97702
start2finish.org

Printed in the United States of America

30 29 28 27 26 1 2 3 4 5

To every young man who, earnestly desiring to preach the Word, has put his hand to the plow and not looked back.

Your labor will not be in vain in the Lord.

"Guard the good deposit entrusted to you."

CONTENTS

INTRODUCTION

Have you ever gotten a text or a letter from someone at exactly the moment you needed it most? Maybe it was a friend reminding you that you're not alone. Maybe it was a parent leaving a note in your lunchbox on a day they knew would be hard. Maybe it was a coach sending a message before the biggest game of your life.

Now imagine getting that kind of message from someone who knows they're about to die, someone who's writing to you from a prison cell, and the words they choose are the last words they'll ever write. That changes things. You'd read every sentence differently. You'd pay attention to every word, because you'd know this person used their final breath to say something they believed mattered more than anything else.

That's what we have in 1–2 Timothy and Titus. Three letters from the apostle Paul to two young men he loved like sons. These are some of the most personal, urgent, and practical pages in the entire New Testament. And at least one of them, 2 Timothy, was written by a man who knew the executioner's sword was coming.

THE MAN BEHIND THE LETTERS

Paul was once the church's most dangerous enemy. He'd hunted down Christians, thrown them in prison, and voted for their deaths. Then Jesus met him on a road to Damascus and turned his life inside out. The persecutor became a preacher. For roughly thirty years after that encounter, Paul traveled the Roman world planting churches, teaching the gospel, and writing letters that would become the backbone of the New Testament.

By the time he wrote these three letters, Paul was near the end. He'd been beaten, stoned, shipwrecked, betrayed, and imprisoned. He'd planted churches across an empire. And now, in the final chapter of his life, he had one consuming concern: what would happen to the gospel after he was gone?

TWO MEN, TWO MISSIONS

Timothy was Paul's most trusted protégé. The son of a Jewish mother and a Greek father, Timothy had grown up in the city of Lystra, where he may have witnessed Paul being stoned and left for dead during his first missionary journey. When Paul came back through Lystra a few years later, he recruited Timothy to join him. From that point on, Timothy traveled with Paul, learned from Paul, and became Paul's go-to man for the toughest assignments. Paul called him "my true child in the faith."

But Timothy was also, by all appearances, young and naturally timid. He faced opposition from older critics who didn't take him seriously. He dealt with stomach problems and frequent illness. And now Paul had stationed him in Ephesus, one of the largest and most important cities in the Roman Empire, to deal with a crisis of false teaching that was tearing the church apart.

Titus was Paul's other key partner. A full Gentile (not half-Jewish like Timothy), Titus had proven himself through difficult diplomatic missions, including a particularly tense assignment in Corinth. Now Paul had left him on the island of Crete, a place with such a bad reputation for lying and laziness that one of its own poets had called the Cretans "always liars, evil beasts, lazy gluttons." Titus' job was to appoint qualified leaders in every town, silence the false teachers, and help these young churches grow up in the faith.

Neither Timothy nor Titus was a permanent local church leader. They were apostolic delegates, special representatives sent by Paul to handle urgent situations. Think of them as field commanders operating under Paul's authority, doing the work Paul could no longer do himself.

WHY THESE LETTERS MATTER

These three letters are sometimes called the "Pastoral Epistles" because they deal so heavily with the care and organization of churches. But they're about much more than church business. At their core, they're about what it takes to keep the gospel alive from one generation to the next.

Paul saw the threats clearly. False teachers were twisting the truth, mixing the gospel with myths and speculations. Church leaders were needed who could teach sound doctrine and model godly character. Believers needed to know how to live in a way that made the gospel attractive to outsiders. And someone had to pick up the torch when Paul was gone.

These letters are Paul's answer to all of those challenges. They cover everything from how to choose church leaders to how to handle money, from the role of Scripture to the nature of salvation, from how to deal with false teachers to how to treat older people and younger people with respect. They're wildly practical. And underneath all the practical instruction runs the deep current of the gospel itself, a gospel that Paul summarizes in some of the most beautiful language he ever wrote.

WHAT YOU'RE ABOUT TO READ

This book divides into three sections following Paul's three letters.

First Timothy (Chapters 1–6) finds Paul writing to Timothy in Ephesus. False teachers have invaded the church, and Paul gives Timothy a blueprint for restoring order. You'll read about the danger of twisted doctrine, the power of prayer, what makes a leader worth following, the call to train yourself for godliness, how to care for the vulnerable, and what it means to live a Christ-shaped life in a world that's pulling you in every other direction.

Second Timothy (Chapters 7–10) is Paul's final letter, written from a Roman prison. This is the most personal of the three. Paul knows he's about to die, and every word carries the weight of a man saying goodbye. He urges Timothy to fan the flame of his gift, to endure hardship like a good soldier, to trust the Scriptures that have equipped him since childhood, and to preach the word no matter what. The famous declaration "I have fought the good fight, I have finished the race, I have kept the faith" comes from here. It is, quite simply, one of the most powerful chapters in the Bible.

Titus (Chapters 11–13) shifts the scene to the island of Crete. Paul writes to Titus with instructions for appointing leaders, silencing deceivers, teaching every group in the church what godly living looks like, and understanding the salvation that makes it all possible. The letter contains one of Paul's clearest summaries of the gospel: "He saved us, not because of works done by us in righteousness, but according to his own mercy."

BEFORE WE BEGIN

One thing to know before you start: these letters were written in a world very different from ours. Slavery was a fact of life. Women had far fewer rights than they do today. Church structures were still being formed. Paul addresses all of these realities, and some of what he says may feel unfamiliar or challenging. When it does, remember that Paul is writing to specific people in specific situations, and his instructions are always shaped by the gospel's call to love, dignity, and truth.

These letters are not dusty relics from a dead religion. They're marching orders for a living faith. They answer the question every generation has to face: how do we guard the truth, live it out, and pass it on?

Paul answered that question with his life. Timothy and Titus answered it with theirs. Now it's your turn.

Turn the page.

1

WHEN THE TRUTH GETS TWISTED

Have you ever seen the movie *Goosebumps*? Not the TV show, but the 2015 film with Jack Black playing the famous horror author R.L. Stine. The whole plot kicks off when a teenager named Zach accidentally opens one of Stine's original manuscripts and releases the monsters from the stories into the real world. Suddenly, a giant praying mantis is tearing through downtown. A werewolf is prowling the neighborhood. The Abominable Snowman of Pasadena is smashing everything in sight. What started as fictional stories on a page have become very real, very dangerous problems.

Here's the thing, though. Those manuscripts looked harmless. They were just books sitting on a shelf. Nobody got hurt as long as the stories stayed where they belonged. But once they got loose, once people started messing with things they shouldn't have been messing with, chaos followed.

That's a pretty good picture of what was happening in the city of Ephesus when Paul wrote his first letter to Timothy. Certain teachers in the church had started spreading ideas that sounded interesting, maybe even spiritual, but were completely disconnected from the truth. They were spinning wild stories, building complicated theories out of Old Testament family trees, and getting everyone tangled up in arguments that went absolutely nowhere. It might have seemed harmless at first. Just some extra Bible study, right? But those ideas were doing real damage. They were pulling people away from the gospel, wrecking their faith, and tearing the church apart from the inside. Paul wrote this letter to make sure Timothy knew exactly what to do about it.

Before we get into the letter itself, you need to know who's who.

Paul was an apostle, someone personally chosen and sent by Jesus Christ to spread the gospel. He wasn't a self-appointed teacher. He didn't wake up one morning and decide to start a ministry. God commanded him to do this work. Paul opens the letter by reminding Timothy (and everyone who would hear the letter read aloud in the church) that his authority comes directly from "God our Savior and Christ Jesus our hope." Those titles matter. In the Old Testament, God alone was called the Savior of his people. He was the one who rescued Israel from slavery in Egypt, the one who delivered them from their enemies over and over again. And here Paul applies that same title to the God who sent him. The rescue mission hasn't changed. The Savior is still saving.

Timothy was a younger man whom Paul had mentored in the faith. Paul calls him "my true child in the faith," which tells you something about how close they were. Timothy wasn't Paul's biological son, but Paul had shaped his faith, trained him, and trusted him with enormous responsibility. Now

Timothy was stationed in Ephesus, one of the largest and most important cities in the Roman Empire, and he had a job to do: protect the church from false teaching.

That job was harder than it sounds.

The false teachers in Ephesus weren't standing on street corners yelling crazy things. They were inside the church. They wanted to be known as experts in God's law, but Paul says they didn't actually understand what they were talking about. They were obsessed with "myths and endless genealogies," which probably means they were taking Old Testament family trees and weaving elaborate stories and theories around them, filling in gaps with speculation and imagination. Think of it like fan fiction for the Bible. They were making up backstories, spinning out complicated ideas, and presenting it all as deep spiritual knowledge.

It might have been fascinating to listen to. New ideas usually are. But Paul says it promoted "speculation rather than God's plan, which operates by faith." In other words, all that creative theorizing wasn't producing anything good. It wasn't drawing people closer to God. It wasn't making anyone more loving or faithful or Christ-like. It was just generating arguments.

And that's the test Paul gives us for any teaching: what does it actually produce?

Good teaching, Paul says, has a clear goal. "The aim of our instruction is love that comes from a pure heart, a good conscience, and a sincere faith." That's it. That's the target. If what someone is teaching leads you toward genuine love for God and for other people, if it cleans up your heart and strengthens your trust in God, then it's sound teaching. But if it just fills your head with theories and ties you up in debates? Something has gone wrong.

The false teachers had missed this completely. Paul says they "wandered away" from love and a good conscience and "turned to meaningless talk." They wanted to be impressive. They wanted to sound smart. But they had drifted from the whole point.

WHAT THE LAW WAS ACTUALLY FOR

Part of the problem was that these teachers claimed to be experts in God's law but were using it in a way God never intended. Paul makes a statement that might surprise you: "The law is good, if one uses it properly." Then he explains that the law wasn't designed for people who are already living right. It was designed for "the lawless and rebellious, the ungodly and sinful."

What follows is a list of sins that roughly tracks with the Ten Commandments. Paul names people who dishonor God, people who harm their own parents, murderers, the sexually immoral, slave traders, liars, and those who swear to things they know aren't true. He's painting a picture of the kind of behavior the law was meant to expose and condemn.

Then he makes a crucial move. He says this kind of lawbreaking is "contrary to the sound doctrine that conforms to the gospel." Did you catch that? The standard isn't just the law anymore. It's the gospel. Sound doctrine, healthy teaching, is teaching that lines up with the good news about Jesus. The law shows us what's wrong. The gospel shows us how God makes it right.

The false teachers were using the law like a puzzle to be solved, a source of interesting theories and arguments. But God gave the law to show people their sin and point them toward a Savior. If you miss that, you've missed everything.

THE WORST SINNER IN THE ROOM

This is where Paul does something unexpected. Instead of continuing to hammer the false teachers, he turns the spotlight on himself.

"I thank Christ Jesus our Lord, who has given me strength, that he considered me trustworthy, appointing me to his service." So far, so good. But then: "Even though I was formerly a blasphemer, a persecutor, and a violent man."

Paul is not exaggerating. Before he met Jesus on the road to Damascus, Paul had made it his personal mission to destroy the church. He dragged Christians out of their homes. He approved of their executions. He spoke against Jesus with hatred and contempt. If you had asked anyone in the early church to name the person least likely to become a follower of Jesus, Paul's name would have been at the top of the list.

But God had mercy on him. Paul says he received mercy because he "acted in ignorance and unbelief." That doesn't mean his actions weren't terrible. It means he didn't fully understand what he was doing. He thought he was serving God when he was actually fighting against him. And even in the middle of all that confusion and violence, God's grace reached him.

Then comes one of the most famous sentences Paul ever wrote: "Christ Jesus came into the world to save sinners, of whom I am the worst."

Paul introduces this statement with a phrase that shows up five times across these three letters: "Here is a trustworthy saying that deserves full acceptance." Whenever you see that phrase, pay attention. Paul is about to say something that the early church considered so important, so central to the faith, that it was probably repeated in worship and memorized by Christians. This is the gospel boiled down to its simplest form. Jesus came. He came into the world. He came to save sinners.

And notice that Paul doesn't say "of whom I *was* the worst." He says "of whom I *am* the worst." Even years after his conversion, Paul never stopped being amazed that God saved someone like him. He never lost his sense of wonder at grace.

Why does Paul tell this story here, in a letter about false teaching? Because his own life is proof that the gospel works. If God's grace could transform a violent persecutor of the church into the greatest missionary the world has ever known, then nothing is too hard for the gospel. Timothy didn't need clever arguments to fight false teaching. He needed the power of the true message: that Christ Jesus came into the world to save sinners.

Paul is so overwhelmed by this truth that he breaks into praise: "Now to the King eternal, immortal, invisible, the only God, be honor and glory for ever and ever. Amen." He can't help it. When you really understand what God has done for you, worship is the only reasonable response.

FIGHT THE GOOD FIGHT

Paul closes the chapter by turning directly to Timothy. "Timothy, my son, I am giving you this instruction in keeping with the prophecies once made about you, so that by recalling them you may fight the good fight."

When Timothy first entered ministry, prophets in the church had spoken over him, confirming that God had called him to this work. Paul wants Timothy to remember those words. Why? Because the fight ahead is going to be hard, and Timothy needs to know that he's not doing this on his own strength. God called him. God equipped him. God will sustain him.

Paul tells Timothy to hold on to two things: "faith and a good conscience." Those two go together. What you believe and how you live are never separate. Your convictions shape your conduct, and your conduct either confirms or contradicts your convictions. If you let go of one, you'll eventually lose the other.

That's exactly what happened to two men Paul names: Hymenaeus and Alexander. They rejected a good conscience, and as a result they "shipwrecked their faith." That's a vivid image, especially for people living in a world where Mediterranean shipwrecks were common and terrifying. A ship that hits the rocks doesn't just spring a leak. It's destroyed. Everything onboard is lost.

Paul says he "handed them over to Satan." That sounds intense, and it is. Most likely, this means Paul removed them from the church community as an act of discipline. The church was God's household, a place of safety and truth. To be put outside it was to be back in the domain where Satan operates. But even this severe action had a purpose: "so that they may learn not to blaspheme." The goal wasn't destruction. It was repentance. Paul wanted them to come to their senses and return.

That's the balance Paul strikes in this chapter. Truth matters enough to fight for. But the fight is always for people, not against them. The goal of good teaching is love. Even discipline is motivated by the hope that the wanderer will come home.

WHAT THIS MEANS FOR US

First, not every idea about God is a good idea. The false teachers in Ephesus sounded spiritual. They probably thought they were doing deep, important work. But because their ideas didn't line up with the gospel, they were actually pulling people away from God. Just because something sounds interesting or religious doesn't mean it's true. The test is always: does this teaching point me toward Jesus and produce love, or does it just generate arguments and confusion?

Second, the gospel is for the worst sinners, not just the respectable ones. Paul didn't clean up his life and then come to Jesus. Jesus came to him while he was still a violent enemy of the faith. If the gospel could save Paul, it can save anyone. That means nobody you know is beyond hope, and it means you never have to pretend to be better than you are in order to come to God.

Third, what you believe and how you live are connected. Hymenaeus and Alexander didn't just adopt some wrong ideas. They rejected their conscience, and their faith fell apart as a result. If you ignore what you know is right, eventually you'll stop believing what's true. Guarding your conscience is guarding your faith.

Fourth, fighting for the truth is an act of love. It might not feel that way. Nobody enjoys confrontation. But when someone is teaching things that lead people away from God, staying quiet isn't kindness. It's neglect. Timothy's job was to protect the church by holding firmly to the gospel, and that's a responsibility every generation of Christians shares.

TALKING POINTS

1. **Paul says the goal of good teaching is "love that comes from a pure heart, a good conscience, and a sincere faith."** Why do you think he puts love as the goal instead of, say, knowledge or being right about everything? What's the difference between knowing a lot about the Bible and actually loving God and other people?

2. **The false teachers in Ephesus wanted to be seen as experts.** Why do you think it's tempting to use religious knowledge to impress people rather than to serve them? Have you ever seen someone use what they know to make others feel small?

3. **Paul calls himself "the worst of sinners" even though he'd been following Jesus for years by the time he wrote this.** Why do you think he still described himself that way? What does that tell us about how we should think about our own sin and God's grace?

4. **Paul told Timothy to "fight the good fight" by holding on to faith and a good conscience.** What do you think it looks like practically for someone your age to "fight the good fight"? What are some situations where you might have to stand up for what's true even when it's uncomfortable?

5. **Hymenaeus and Alexander "shipwrecked their faith" by rejecting their conscience.** Can you think of a time when you knew something was wrong but were tempted to ignore that feeling? Why is it important to listen to your conscience, and how can you tell the difference between a guilty conscience and just feeling nervous?

Timothy's assignment was clear: stay in Ephesus, protect the truth, and never forget that the gospel is the most powerful force in the world. But the letter was just getting started. Paul had a lot more to say about what a healthy church looks like, and it begins with something you might not expect: prayer.

Turn the page.

2

PRAYERS FOR EVERYONE

George Orwell's novel *1984* imagines the most terrifying government you could dream up. The story takes place in a country ruled by a figure called Big Brother, whose face stares down from posters on every wall. The government watches everything its citizens do. It controls what people read, what they say, even what they think. If you disagree with Big Brother, you don't just get punished. You disappear. The main character, Winston, lives in constant fear, surrounded by propaganda, knowing that the people in power see him as nothing more than a tool to be used or a threat to be eliminated.

Now imagine someone handing you a letter that says: "Pray for Big Brother. Pray for his officials. Pray for their salvation."

You'd probably think the person had lost their mind. Why would you pray for someone who oppresses you? Why waste your breath asking God to bless the people making your life miserable?

And yet that's almost exactly what Paul told the Christians in Ephesus to do. The Roman Empire in the first century wasn't as extreme as Orwell's fictional nightmare, but it was close enough. The emperor claimed divine honors. Roman officials could make life very difficult for anyone who refused to worship the empire's gods. Christians were a tiny, vulnerable minority in a world that didn't understand them and often didn't want them around.

Into that situation, Paul writes: pray for everyone. Including the people in charge. Including the ones who might be your enemies.

Why? Because God wants everyone to be saved. Even them.

Paul opens 1 Timothy 2 with an urgent instruction. "First of all," he writes, "I urge that supplications, prayers, intercessions, and thanksgivings be made for all people." He stacks up four different words for prayer, and the effect is like saying, "Pray in every way you can think of, and do it for *everyone*."

Then he gets specific: "for kings and all who are in high positions." Remember, the "king" for Paul's readers was the Roman emperor. This wasn't some friendly elected official. This was a ruler who sat at the top of the most powerful empire on earth, who was worshiped as a god by his subjects, and who had the authority to imprison or execute anyone he chose. Paul himself was writing from personal experience. He had been arrested, beaten, and jailed by Roman authorities. He would eventually be executed by them.

And his instruction to the church? Pray for them.

But not just so they'd leave the Christians alone. Paul gives a deeper reason: pray "that we may lead a peaceful and quiet life, godly and dignified in every way." The goal wasn't comfort for its own sake. A peaceful society was one where the gospel could spread freely. When civic life was calm, when there was no persecution or violence disrupting daily existence, Christians could go about the work God had given them: sharing the good news with everyone they could reach.

Paul connects the dots: "This is good, and it is pleasing in the sight of God our Savior, who desires all people to be saved and to come to the knowledge of the truth."

Stop and read that sentence again. God desires *all* people to be saved. Not just the good ones. Not just the Jewish ones. Not just the ones who already seem interested. All people. The Roman soldier who guards the prison door. The emperor who sits on the throne. The merchant down the street who worships a dozen different gods. The slave who has never heard the name of Jesus. God's desire for salvation has no boundaries.

This was a radical idea, and Paul knew it. Some of the false teachers in Ephesus may have been promoting a version of faith that was exclusive, one that suggested salvation was only for certain kinds of people, perhaps only for those who had the right ancestry or the right special knowledge. Paul blows that idea apart. God's rescue plan isn't for a select club. It's for the whole world.

ONE GOD, ONE MEDIATOR

To support this enormous claim, Paul reaches for one of the most important theological statements in all his letters: "For there is one God, and there is one mediator between God and mankind, the man Christ Jesus, who gave himself as a ransom for all."

There's a lot packed into those few words. Let's break it down.

One God. This echoes the foundational Jewish confession from Deuteronomy 6:4: "Hear, O Israel: the Lord our God, the Lord is one." There aren't many gods competing for territory, each one saving a different group of people. There is one God over the entire universe, and his plan of salvation is for all of humanity.

One mediator. A mediator is someone who stands between two parties and brings them together. Think of it like a translator who speaks both languages. Humanity is separated from God by sin, and we have no way to bridge that gap on our own. We need someone who can represent both sides, someone who is both fully God and fully human. That someone is Jesus.

Paul calls him "the man Christ Jesus." He's emphasizing the humanity of Jesus here, not because Jesus isn't God (Paul has already called him Lord and placed him alongside the Father), but because it was by becoming human that Jesus was able to stand in our place. He lived the life we couldn't live. He bridged the gap we couldn't cross.

A ransom for all. The word "ransom" comes from the world of slavery. In the ancient world, a ransom was the price paid to set a captive free. If you were a prisoner of war or a slave, someone could buy your freedom by paying the ransom price. Paul says that's what Jesus did. We were held captive by sin and death, completely unable to free ourselves, and Jesus paid the price with his own life. He "gave himself" willingly. Nobody forced him. He chose to die so that we could go free.

And this ransom was "for all." Not for some. Not for a chosen few. For all.

Paul then reminds Timothy that this is exactly why God made him an apostle: "For this I was appointed a herald and an apostle, a teacher of the Gentiles in faith and truth." Paul's entire ministry was living proof that God's salvation extended beyond Israel to every nation on earth. The former persecutor of the church was now its greatest missionary, carrying the message to people who had never heard it.

Do you see how it all connects? There is one God, so there can only be one way of salvation. There is one mediator, Jesus, who gave himself for all people. Therefore the church must pray for all people and share the gospel with all people. The logic is airtight. If God desires every person to be saved, then the church has no business writing anyone off as unreachable or unworthy.

HOW MEN AND WOMEN WORSHIP

In the second half of the chapter, Paul shifts from the mission of the church to the behavior of its members when they gather for worship. He addresses men and women separately, giving each group instructions that fit the challenges they were facing.

To the men, Paul says: "I desire that in every place the men should pray, lifting holy hands without anger or quarreling." The image of lifting hands in prayer was common in the ancient world, both in Jewish worship and in the surrounding culture. But Paul's emphasis isn't on the posture. It's on the character behind it. The hands must be "holy," meaning the person praying must be living a life that matches their prayers. And they must come to God "without anger or quarreling," which suggests that some of the men in the Ephesian church were bringing their personal conflicts into the worship assembly. You can't pray for the whole world while holding a grudge against the person sitting next to you.

To the women, Paul gives instructions about appearance and attitude. "Women should adorn themselves in respectable apparel, with modesty and self-control, not with braided hair and gold or pearls or costly attire, but with what is proper for women who profess godliness: good works."

This might sound strange to modern ears, but it made perfect sense in first-century Ephesus. Elaborate hairstyles, expensive jewelry, and luxurious clothing were markers of wealth and social status. When women showed up to worship dressed to impress, it created division between rich and poor, distracted from the purpose of the gathering, and sent a terrible message to any outsiders who might be watching. Paul isn't saying that women can't look nice. He's saying that the real beauty of a Christian woman is found in her character and her service, not in how much money she spends on her appearance.

Paul then addresses a sensitive topic: women learning and teaching in the church assembly. He writes, "Let a woman learn quietly with all submissiveness. I do not permit a woman to teach or to exercise authority over a man; she must be quiet."

This is one of the most discussed passages in all of Paul's letters. To understand what Paul is saying, we need to keep a few things in mind.

First, Paul affirms that women should *learn*. In the ancient world, this wasn't a given. Many cultures didn't think women needed to be educated at all. Paul insists they do. They are to be taught the faith alongside the men.

Second, Paul roots his instruction in the creation account from Genesis. He points out that Adam was formed first, then Eve, and that Eve was the one deceived by the serpent. Paul isn't saying women are less intelligent or more easily fooled than men. He's saying that God designed an order for his household, an order established at creation, not invented by any human culture. In that order, the responsibility for leading and teaching in the gathered church belongs to qualified men.

Third, remember the situation in Ephesus. Some women in the church appear to have been disrupting the teaching, possibly under the influence of the false teachers Paul warned about in chapter 1. Paul's instructions address both the immediate problem and the deeper principle behind it.

Paul closes the section with a difficult verse: women "will be saved through childbearing, if they continue in faith and love and holiness, with self-control." This doesn't mean women earn salvation by having babies. Paul has just finished explaining that salvation comes through Christ alone. The word "saved" here likely carries the sense of being preserved or kept safe. Paul is saying that women who embrace their God-given roles, symbolized here by the domestic sphere of home and family, and who continue in faith and love and holiness, will be kept safe from the deception and disorder that was plaguing the church. The path of faithfulness, not the path of the false teachers, is the one that leads to life.

WHAT THIS MEANS FOR US

First, prayer is the engine of mission. Paul doesn't tell the church to start a political campaign or organize a protest march. He tells them to pray. Prayer for all people, including leaders and rulers, is the foundation of the church's outreach to the world. If you want to change the world, start on your knees.

Second, nobody is beyond the reach of God's love. God desires all people to be saved. That includes the bully at school, the neighbor who's rude to your family, the world leader who makes decisions you disagree with, and the person you've written off as hopeless. If God hasn't given up on them, neither should we.

Third, how you present yourself matters. Paul's instructions about clothing and behavior aren't about following a dress code. They're about making sure that nothing about your life distracts from the gospel. Whether it's showing off your clothes, losing your temper in public, or trying to dominate others, anything that draws attention to yourself and away from Jesus is working against the mission.

Fourth, God's design for men and women is rooted in creation, not culture. Paul doesn't argue from the customs of his day. He argues from Genesis. Men and women are equally valuable, equally saved, equally loved by God, but they have different roles in the household of God. Understanding and embracing those differences isn't a limitation. It's part of God's good design for how his people flourish.

TALKING POINTS

1. **Paul says to pray for "kings and all who are in high positions."** What would it look like for you to regularly pray for leaders in your community, your country, or the world? How might praying for someone change the way you think about them?

2. **The statement "God desires all people to be saved" is one of the most sweeping claims in the Bible.** Is there anyone

in your life you've secretly thought was too far gone for God to reach? How does this verse challenge that assumption?

3. **Paul says there is "one mediator between God and mankind, the man Christ Jesus."** Why do you think it matters that Jesus is both fully God and fully human? What would be missing if he were only one or the other?

4. **Paul tells men to pray "without anger or quarreling" and tells women to focus on good works rather than expensive appearance.** What are some ways that conflict or showing off might distract a church from its mission today?

5. **Paul grounds his instructions for men and women in the story of Adam and Eve from Genesis.** Why do you think he goes all the way back to creation instead of just giving practical advice? What does this tell us about how seriously God takes the design of his household?

Paul has laid out the mission of the church (pray for everyone, because God wants everyone saved) and the character of its members (holiness, humility, and order). But a mission this important needs trustworthy leaders. Who should run God's household? What kind of people should they be? That's where Paul goes next.

Turn the page.

3

LEADERS WORTH FOLLOWING

The 2003 comedy *Cheaper by the Dozen* follows the Baker family, a household with twelve kids. When the father, Tom, lands his dream job as a college football coach, the family moves to a new city, and everything immediately starts to unravel. The kids are miserable at their new schools. The house descends into chaos. One son runs away. Another gets into fights. The youngest feels completely lost. Meanwhile, Tom is so consumed with his new coaching position that he barely notices his family falling apart around him.

The turning point comes when Tom realizes something important: it doesn't matter how successful he is at work if he's failing at home. He can draw up brilliant plays and inspire a football team, but if his own kids are hurting and his family is in shambles, none of that success means anything. The job isn't worth losing his family over.

Paul would have loved that movie. Not because he cared about football, but because the lesson at the heart of the story is the exact same lesson at the heart of 1 Timothy 3. When Paul lays out what kind of person should lead the church, the first place he looks isn't at their resume, their public speaking skills, or their Bible knowledge. He looks at their home. Because if you can't lead your family well, Paul says, you have no business trying to lead God's family.

Paul opens this chapter with another "trustworthy saying," the kind of statement that the early church had already recognized as reliable and important: "If anyone aspires to the office of overseer, he desires a noble task."

The word "overseer" describes someone who watches over, cares for, and manages a group of Christians. In the New Testament, "overseer" and "elder" refer to the same role. These were the primary leaders of the local church. And Paul wants everyone to know that wanting this role is a good thing. It's not arrogant to desire it. Leading God's people is a noble task, a beautiful responsibility.

But wanting it isn't enough. The rest of the chapter is Paul's answer to the question: what kind of person should an overseer be?

THE CHARACTER OF AN OVERSEER

What's striking about Paul's list of qualifications is what *isn't* on it. He doesn't mention preaching ability (except a brief reference to being "able to teach"). He doesn't mention charisma or vision or organizational skills. He doesn't ask whether the person is dynamic or popular or good on a stage.

Almost everything on the list is about character.

"An overseer must be above reproach." That's the headline, and everything that follows fills in what it means. To be "above reproach" isn't the same as being perfect. It means that when people look at your life, they can't point to anything that would bring shame on the church or undermine your ability to lead.

Here's what Paul lists:

Faithful to his wife. The overseer must be a man committed to his marriage. In the culture of Paul's day, it was common for married men to be unfaithful. Visiting prostitutes or having affairs was considered normal in much of the Roman world. But the church was to be different. A leader of God's people had to model faithfulness in his closest human relationship.

Self-controlled, respectable, hospitable. These three qualities paint a picture of a steady, dignified person who opens his home to others. In the ancient world, churches met in homes, so hospitality wasn't just a nice bonus for a leader. It was essential. An overseer who wouldn't open his door to others couldn't very well open the church to them.

Able to teach. This is the one "skill" on the list, and it's crucial. The overseer's primary job was to teach sound doctrine and correct false teaching. He didn't have to be the most eloquent speaker in the room, but he had to know the faith well enough to explain it clearly and defend it when it came under attack. In a church plagued by false teachers (like the ones Paul described in chapter 1), this ability was a matter of survival.

Not a drunkard, not violent but gentle, not quarrelsome. Paul has a specific picture in mind: a man who doesn't lose control. Drunkenness leads to poor decisions. Violence and quarreling destroy trust. The false teachers were characterized by arrogance and arguing (6:4). The overseer was to be the exact opposite: calm, gentle, and reasonable. The kind of person people actually want to follow.

Not a lover of money. Since overseers likely handled money for the church and hosted gatherings in their homes, the temptation to use the position for financial gain was real. Paul is blunt: if you're in it for the money, you're disqualified.

THE HOME TEST

Then comes the qualification Paul develops the most: "He must manage his own household well, having his children submit to him with all reverence." And in case anyone misses the point, Paul spells out the logic: "For if someone does not know how to manage his own household, how will he care for God's church?"

This is the Tom Baker principle. Your home is the proving ground for your leadership. The way you treat your spouse, the way you raise your children, the way you handle conflict and money and daily responsibilities under your own roof reveals who you really are. Public ministry is a performance anyone can put on for a few hours a week. Private life is where your true character shows.

Paul uses the word "manage" here, but it means more than just keeping things organized. It includes the ideas of leading, caring for, and protecting. A father who manages his household well isn't a dictator barking orders. He's a shepherd who leads his family with love, earns their respect, and creates an environment where everyone flourishes.

If that sounds familiar, it should. It's the same thing God does for his people.

TWO MORE GUARDRAILS

Paul adds two final qualifications. First, the overseer "must not be a recent convert, or he may become puffed up with conceit and fall into the condemnation of the devil." A brand-new Christian hasn't had time to develop the maturity or humility that leadership demands. Putting someone in charge too soon can inflate their ego, and pride, Paul warns, is the very thing that brought down the devil himself.

Second, "he must be well thought of by outsiders, so that he may not fall into disgrace and into a snare of the devil." The overseer's reputation with people outside the church matters too. If unbelievers know him as dishonest, hot-tempered, or shady in his business dealings, his leadership will be a stumbling block to the gospel. The church's mission depends partly on its leaders being people that even non-Christians can respect.

DEACONS: SERVANTS OF THE CHURCH

After the overseer qualifications, Paul turns to a second leadership role: deacons. The word "deacon" means "servant" or "helper." Deacons assisted the overseers in caring for the church and its practical needs. Think of them as the people who made sure the work actually got done.

Their qualifications overlap significantly with those of overseers. They must be dignified, sincere in their speech, not heavy drinkers, not greedy, and tested before they serve. They must manage their households well. And they must "hold the mystery of the faith with a clear conscience," meaning they must genuinely believe and live out the gospel, not just go through the motions.

Paul ends the section with an encouragement: "Those who serve well as deacons gain a good standing for themselves and great confidence in the faith that is in Christ Jesus." Faithful service doesn't go unnoticed. It builds trust, deepens faith, and earns the respect of the community.

THE PILLAR AND FOUNDATION OF THE TRUTH

Paul now steps back and reveals why all of this matters so much. He tells Timothy, "I am writing these things to you so that you may know how one ought to behave in the household of God, which is the church of the living God, a pillar and buttress of the truth."

Three images for the church are packed into that sentence.

The *household of God*: the church is a family. God is the Father. Christians are brothers and sisters. The overseers and deacons aren't corporate executives running a business. They're family members caring for a home.

The *church of the living God*: unlike the dead idols of Ephesus (the city was famous for its massive temple to the goddess Artemis), the God who dwells in this community is alive. He speaks. He acts. He saves.

The *pillar and buttress of the truth*: just as pillars hold up a building, the church holds up the truth of the gospel. Without the church faithfully teaching, defending, and living out the truth, that truth would be lost to the world. This is why leadership matters so desperately. Bad leaders let the pillars crumble.

THE GREAT MYSTERY

Paul closes the chapter with what appears to be an early Christian hymn or confession. He calls it “the mystery of godliness,” meaning the revealed truth at the heart of the faith: “He was manifested in the flesh, vindicated by the Spirit, seen by angels, proclaimed among the nations, believed on in the world, taken up in glory.”

Six lines. Six massive truths about Jesus. He became human. He was raised from the dead by the Spirit. Angels witnessed his resurrection. The gospel went out to every nation. People all over the world believed. And he ascended to heaven in glory.

This is what the church exists to protect and proclaim. This is the truth that the pillars are holding up. This is why overseers must be people of character, why deacons must be people of integrity, and why Timothy couldn’t afford to let the false teachers win. The stakes were nothing less than the gospel itself.

WHAT THIS MEANS FOR US

First, character matters more than talent. The world picks leaders based on skill, charisma, and confidence. God picks leaders based on faithfulness, self-control, gentleness, and integrity. If you want to be the kind of person who leads well someday, start building your character now. How you treat people when nobody’s watching matters more than how you perform when everybody is.

Second, your home reveals your heart. Paul says the family is the training ground for church leadership. That means how you act at home—toward your parents, your siblings, and in your daily responsibilities—is a window into who you really are. Anyone can act one way at church and another way at home. Integrity means being the same person in both places.

Third, the church is a family, not a business. When Paul calls the church "the household of God," he's not using corporate language. He's using family language. That means the church should feel like a place where you belong, where people care for each other, and where leaders serve with the same kind of love a good parent shows a child.

Fourth, the gospel is worth protecting. The church is called "the pillar and foundation of the truth." That's an enormous responsibility. Every generation of Christians is entrusted with the same message: Jesus came in the flesh, died for sinners, rose from the dead, and was taken up in glory. If the church stops teaching that truth, the world stops hearing it.

TALKING POINTS

1. **Paul's list of qualifications for overseers is almost entirely about character, not skills.** Why do you think character matters more than ability when it comes to leading God's people? Can you think of a time when someone's character (good or bad) affected how well they led?

2. **Paul says that managing your household well is the proving ground for managing God's church.** What do you think "managing a household well" looks like? How might that apply to the responsibilities you have right now, even as a young person?

3. **The overseer must not be "a recent convert."** Why do you think spiritual maturity matters for leadership? What's the danger of putting someone in charge too quickly?

4. **Paul calls the church "the pillar and buttress of the truth."** What do you think it means for the church to hold up

the truth? What happens when a church stops doing that?

5. **The chapter ends with a hymn about Jesus: manifested in the flesh, vindicated by the Spirit, proclaimed among the nations, believed in the world, taken up in glory.** Which line of this hymn stands out to you the most, and why?

Paul has shown Timothy what the church is and what kind of people should lead it. But there's a threat on the horizon. False teaching isn't just a past problem. Paul sees it coming in the future too, and he has urgent advice for how Timothy should prepare.

Turn the page.

4

TRAIN YOURSELF FOR GODLINESS

Stephen Crane's novel *The Red Badge of Courage* tells the story of Henry Fleming, a young man who enlists in the Union army during the Civil War. Henry is desperate to prove himself, but he's terrified. He has no idea what real battle will be like. He wonders if he'll stand his ground when the shooting starts or if he'll turn and run.

When his first real fight comes, Henry does the worst thing he can imagine: he panics and flees. He runs through the woods, sick with shame, convinced he's a coward. But the story doesn't end there. Over the days that follow, Henry slowly finds his courage. He watches other soldiers face their fear. He picks up a fallen flag and carries it forward. He learns that bravery isn't the absence of fear. It's the decision to keep going anyway. By the end of the book, Henry has become the soldier he wanted to be, not because the fear went away, but because he trained himself to act in spite of it.

Paul's message to Timothy in 1 Timothy 4 carries a similar idea. Timothy was young. He was outnumbered by false teachers. People may have doubted him because of his age. And the work ahead of him was going to be hard, discouraging, and exhausting. Paul's solution wasn't to tell Timothy to wait until he felt ready. It was to tell him to start training. "Train yourself for godliness," Paul writes. Spiritual maturity doesn't happen by accident. It's built through discipline, practice, and perseverance—the same way a soldier is forged through drills and battles, not by sitting around hoping courage will show up on its own.

Paul opens the chapter with a warning. "The Spirit expressly says that in later times some will depart from the faith by devoting themselves to deceitful spirits and teachings of demons."

This sounds dramatic, and it is. Paul is saying that the false teaching threatening the Ephesian church isn't just bad theology. It has a spiritual source. Behind the human teachers spreading confusion, there are demonic forces at work, deceiving people and pulling them away from the truth.

How does this deception show up? Paul gives two specific examples. The false teachers "forbid marriage and require abstinence from foods that God created to be received with thanksgiving."

Both of these restrictions are attacks on God's creation. Marriage was established by God in Genesis and declared good. Food was created by God and given to humanity as a gift. The false teachers were essentially saying, "If you want to be really spiritual, you need to deny yourself these things. Stay away from marriage. Stay away from certain foods." It sounded deeply religious. It sounded like serious commitment. But it was actually an insult to the Creator.

Paul's response is simple and powerful: "For everything created by God is good, and nothing is to be rejected if it is received with thanksgiving, for it is made holy by the word of God and prayer."

Read that slowly. *Everything* created by God is good. *Nothing* is to be rejected. The proper response to God's good gifts isn't to avoid them. It's to receive them with gratitude. When you sit down to eat and thank God for the food on your plate, that act of thanksgiving recognizes God as the giver. It makes the ordinary sacred. A meal eaten with gratitude is an act of worship.

The false teachers had it exactly backward. They thought spirituality meant rejecting the physical world. Paul says true spirituality means receiving the physical world as a gift from God's hand and saying thank you.

JUNK FOOD AND REAL FOOD

Paul now turns directly to Timothy. "If you put these things before the brothers and sisters, you will be a good servant of Christ Jesus, nourished on the words of the faith and of the sound teaching that you have followed."

Notice the word "nourished." Paul is comparing sound doctrine to food. Just as your body needs real nutrition to grow strong, your soul needs truth. Timothy has been feeding on the right stuff: the apostolic teaching, the words of faith, the sound doctrine Paul handed down to him. That's his spiritual diet, and it's what qualifies him to feed others.

But there's also junk food available. "Have nothing to do with irreverent, silly myths," Paul says. The word he uses for "silly" literally suggests the kind of ridiculous stories that nobody should take seriously. These are the speculative tales and genealogical theories the false teachers loved. They might taste interesting, but they have zero nutritional value. They don't build faith. They don't produce love. They don't grow you closer to God.

Instead of filling up on spiritual junk food, Paul gives Timothy a better assignment: "Train yourself for godliness." The word "train" is an athletic term. Paul's readers would have immediately pictured the gymnasium, the training ground where athletes prepared for competition. The Greek and Roman world was obsessed with athletics. They understood that you don't win a race by wishing. You win by training, by putting in the work day after day, by disciplining your body until it can do what your mind demands.

Paul takes that image and applies it to the spiritual life. "Physical training is of some value," he admits. Staying in shape matters. But "godliness is of value in every way, as it holds promise for the present life and also for the life to come."

Physical fitness benefits you now, in this body, in this life. But spiritual fitness benefits you now *and* forever. An athlete trains for a competition that lasts hours or days. A Christian trains for an eternity. That's why Paul can say, "For to this end we toil and strive, because we have our hope set on the living God, who is the Savior of all people, especially of those who believe."

The "living God" is contrasted with the dead idols of Ephesus. He's not a statue. He's not a theory. He's alive, active, and powerful enough to save anyone who trusts him. And because he is alive and because his promises extend into eternity, the training is worth every ounce of effort.

DON'T LET ANYONE LOOK DOWN ON YOU

Now comes one of the most encouraging passages Paul ever wrote for a young person. "Let no one despise you for your youth, but set the believers an example in speech, in conduct, in love, in faith, in purity."

Timothy was probably in his mid-thirties, which in the ancient world was still considered young for a leadership position. Older members of the church may have looked at him and thought, "What does this kid know?" In a culture that automatically associated authority with age, Timothy faced an uphill battle for respect.

Paul's advice is brilliant. He doesn't tell Timothy to demand respect or pull rank. He doesn't say, "Remind them that I put you in charge." Instead, he says: earn it. Set such a high example that nobody can dismiss you, no matter how young you are. Let your speech be honest and gracious. Let your behavior be consistent. Let your love be genuine. Let your faith be visible. Let your purity be beyond question.

Paul is saying that the best argument for your leadership is your life. If your character is solid, your age becomes irrelevant.

Then Paul gives Timothy three specific duties to focus on until Paul can visit in person: "Devote yourself to the public reading of Scripture, to exhortation, to teaching." These weren't three separate activities. They were one seamless ministry. In the early church (borrowing from the practice of the Jewish synagogue), a passage of Scripture would be read aloud to the congregation, then explained and applied. Timothy was to make sure the word of God was front and center in every gathering. His authority wasn't his own. It was the authority of the text he read and taught.

DON'T NEGLECT YOUR GIFT

"Do not neglect the gift you have, which was given you by prophecy when the council of elders laid their hands on you." At some point in Timothy's ministry, the Holy Spirit had spoken through prophets in the church, confirming Timothy's calling and gifting for ministry. The elders had laid hands on him as a sign of recognition and commissioning. God had given Timothy a specific gift for his specific task, and Paul wants him to use it.

Gifts from God aren't permanent deposits that sit in a vault somewhere. They're more like muscles: if you don't use them, they waste away. Timothy couldn't afford to let fear, discouragement, or the pressure of opposition cause him to pull back from the work God had given him. He had to exercise his gift, develop it, and put it to work.

WATCH YOUR LIFE AND YOUR TEACHING

Paul closes the chapter with a charge that ties everything together: "Practice these things, immerse yourself in them, so that all may see your progress. Keep a close watch on yourself and on the teaching. Persist in this, for by so doing you will save both yourself and your hearers."

Two things stand out. First, Paul expects Timothy's growth to be visible. "So that all may see your progress." Spiritual maturity isn't something you announce. It's something people observe over time. Timothy wasn't expected to be perfect. He was expected to be growing, and growing visibly.

Second, Paul links Timothy's personal faithfulness to the salvation of others. "You will save both yourself and your hearers." This doesn't mean Timothy earns his own salvation by his effort. It means that if Timothy abandons sound teaching or lets his character slip, both he and the people who follow his teaching will suffer the consequences. A leader's life and doctrine are not private matters. Other people's faith depends on them.

That's a sobering thought. But it's also a motivating one. The work Timothy does matters beyond himself. Every time he opens the Scriptures, every time he corrects false teaching, every time he sets a godly example, he's not just helping himself. He's holding the door open for everyone who hears him.

WHAT THIS MEANS FOR US

First, true spirituality doesn't reject God's creation. It receives it with thanksgiving. God made food, marriage, friendships, nature, and the physical world, and he called it all good. When someone tells you that being really spiritual means avoiding good things God created, that's a red flag. Gratitude is the mark of genuine faith.

Second, spiritual growth requires training, not just time. You don't become a godly person by accident, any more than you become a great athlete by watching games on TV. Reading Scripture, praying, practicing self-control, serving others—these are the spiritual exercises that build real character. If you want to be strong in your faith ten years from now, start training today.

Third, your age doesn't determine your influence. Timothy was young, and Paul didn't tell him to wait until he was older.

He told him to live such an impressive life that his age wouldn't matter. If you're a young person who takes your faith seriously, your example can be more powerful than you think. People notice when a teenager chooses integrity over popularity.

Fourth, watch your life and your teaching. What you believe and how you live are two sides of the same coin, and both of them affect the people around you. If your words say one thing and your actions say another, people will always believe your actions. Consistency between what you teach and how you live is the most powerful testimony you have.

TALKING POINTS

1. **The false teachers told people to avoid marriage and certain foods.** Why do you think it's tempting to believe that being "more spiritual" means giving up good things? Have you ever encountered the idea that really devoted Christians should deny themselves things God created to be enjoyed?

2. **Paul compares spiritual training to physical training.** What "exercises" do you think help build spiritual strength? If you were going to design a daily spiritual training plan for yourself, what would be on it?

3. **Paul tells Timothy, "Let no one despise you for your youth."** What does that feel like in your own life? Have you ever been dismissed or overlooked because of your age? How can you follow Paul's advice and set an example even now?

4. **Paul says Timothy's progress should be visible to everyone.** What does spiritual "progress" look like? How can you tell when someone is growing in their faith, compared to just going through the motions?

5. **Paul warns Timothy to "keep a close watch on yourself and on the teaching."** Why do you think he puts "yourself" before "the teaching"? What happens to a leader whose personal life doesn't match what they teach?

Timothy had his marching orders: reject the lies, train for godliness, set the example, and guard both his life and his doctrine. But leadership isn't just about personal discipline. It's also about how you treat the people God has placed in your care. Paul is about to get very practical about what that looks like.

Turn the page.

5

TAKING CARE OF EACH OTHER

The Sound of Music opens with a problem. Captain von Trapp, a widowed naval officer in Austria, has seven children ranging from a teenager to a toddler, and he has no idea how to connect with any of them. He runs his household like a military unit, complete with a whistle to summon the kids and matching uniforms to keep them in line. The children are miserable. They keep driving away every governess he hires because nobody in the house actually treats them like people.

Then Maria shows up. She's messy, unpredictable, and completely out of her depth. But she does one thing that nobody else has done: she pays attention to each child as an individual. She notices that Liesl, the oldest, is a young woman who needs to be trusted, not controlled. She sees that Friedrich is a teenager who needs to be treated with respect. She recognizes that little Gretl just needs to feel safe. Maria doesn't use the same approach with every child because every child is different. She meets each one where they are, and slowly the house transforms from a cold institution into an actual family.

That's essentially what Paul is doing in this section of 1 Timothy. He's already told Timothy that the church is "the household of God" (3:15). Now he gets practical about what that means. A household includes people of every age and situation: older men and women, younger men and women, widows in crisis, leaders who need accountability, and even slaves who need dignity. Each group requires a different kind of care. You don't talk to an older man the same way you talk to a peer. You don't treat a widow with resources the same as a widow with nothing. Leading God's family means learning to see each person clearly and care for them accordingly.

TREAT THE CHURCH LIKE A FAMILY

Paul opens with a simple but important principle: "Do not rebuke an older man harshly, but exhort him as you would a father. Treat younger men as brothers, older women as mothers, younger women as sisters, in all purity."

This is family language, and it's deliberate. When Timothy needs to correct an older man in the church, he shouldn't speak to him the way a boss speaks to an employee. He should speak to him the way a son speaks to a father: with respect, even when the conversation is difficult. When he relates to younger men, he should treat them as brothers, as equals in the family. With older women, he should show the honor and tenderness of a son toward a mother. And with younger women, he must relate as a brother, with absolute purity.

That last phrase matters. Paul knew that a young leader like Timothy would regularly interact with younger women in the church, and he wanted to leave no room for ambiguity.

Those relationships must be marked by the kind of purity and respect that a brother shows a sister. Nothing less.

REAL WIDOWS

The longest section in this passage deals with widows, and it may seem strange that Paul spends so much time on this topic. But in the ancient world, a woman who lost her husband was in serious trouble. There were no government programs, no Social Security checks, no safety net. If a widow had no family to take her in, she could end up destitute, begging on the street to survive. The church had taken on the responsibility of caring for these women, and that was exactly right. But resources were limited, and Paul needed to help Timothy figure out who genuinely needed the church's help and who had other options.

Paul starts with a clear command: "Honor widows who are truly widows." The word "honor" here includes the idea of financial support. The church should provide for women who have no other means of survival.

But some widows did have other options. "If a widow has children or grandchildren," Paul writes, "let them first learn to show godliness to their own household and to make some return to their parents, for this is pleasing in the sight of God." Before the church steps in, the family should step up. Taking care of your aging parents or grandparents isn't just a nice thing to do. Paul calls it an act of godliness, a way of obeying the fifth commandment to honor your father and mother. In fact, Paul is so serious about this that he later says, "If anyone does not provide for his relatives, and especially for members of his household, he has denied the faith and is worse than an unbeliever." That's strong language. But Paul means it. A faith that doesn't take care of family isn't real faith.

The "true widow," the one the church should support, is a woman who is truly alone, with no family to care for her, and who has set her hope on God. She is devoted to prayer. She has a reputation for good works: raising children (possibly including orphans), showing hospitality, caring for the sick, and serving others in every way she could.

Paul sets a minimum age of sixty for the formal support list. He also instructs younger widows to remarry, have children, and manage their homes rather than being enrolled for church support. This wasn't about limiting women. It was about protecting the church's limited resources for those who needed them most, and about encouraging younger women toward productive lives rather than idleness. Paul had seen what happened when younger widows with no purpose began going from house to house, falling into gossip and meddling. Some had even been drawn in by false teachers and strayed from the faith. Marriage, family, and purposeful work would protect them from that danger.

ELDERS WHO LEAD WELL

Paul shifts next to the leaders of the church: the elders. "Let the elders who rule well be considered worthy of double honor," he writes, "especially those who labor in preaching and teaching."

Just as "honor" for widows meant financial support, "double honor" for elders means both respect and compensation. People who devote their lives to preaching and teaching the word of God deserve to be supported. Paul backs this up with two quotations he calls "Scripture." The first is from Deuteronomy: "You shall not muzzle an ox when it treads out the grain." Just as a working animal deserves to eat from the harvest it helps produce, a minister who labors in the word deserves to be supported by the church. The second quote comes from Jesus himself: "The laborer deserves his wages." Paul is placing the words of Jesus on the same level as the Old Testament, which tells us something important about how early the church recognized the authority of Jesus' teachings as Scripture.

But elders are not above accountability. "Do not admit a charge against an elder except on the evidence of two or three witnesses," Paul says, echoing the Old Testament standard for legal proceedings. Leaders shouldn't be taken down by a single disgruntled person's accusation. But when sin is confirmed, Paul is equally firm: "As for those who persist in sin, rebuke them in the presence of all, so that the rest may stand in fear."

This is hard but necessary. When a leader continues sinning and refuses to change, the church can't look the other way. Public accountability protects the church and preserves the integrity of leadership. It also serves as a warning to everyone else: nobody is above God's standards.

Paul then charges Timothy "in the presence of God and of Christ Jesus and of the elect angels" to carry out these instructions "without prejudging, doing nothing from partiality." That's one of the most solemn commands in all of Paul's letters. He invokes the heavenly court as witnesses because he knows how tempting it will be for Timothy to play favorites, to go easy on leaders he likes and come down hard on ones he doesn't. Fairness isn't optional. It's a sacred duty.

DON'T BE HASTY

"Do not be hasty in the laying on of hands," Paul adds. This almost certainly refers to ordaining leaders. Don't rush someone into a position of authority before you've had time to evaluate their character. This connects back to chapter 3: the qualifications for overseers and deacons exist precisely so the church won't put the wrong people in charge.

Paul explains why patience matters: "The sins of some people are conspicuous, going before them to judgment, but the sins of others appear later. So also good works are conspicuous, and even those that are not cannot remain hidden." In other words, what you see on the surface isn't always the whole story. Some people's flaws are obvious immediately. Others look fine at first, but their true character comes out over time. The same is true of good qualities. Patience and careful observation will reveal what a quick decision might miss.

SLAVES AND MASTERS

Paul closes this section with brief instructions for Christian slaves. "Let all who are under the yoke as slaves regard their own masters as worthy of all respect, so that the name of God and the teaching may not be blasphemed."

Slavery was a brutal reality of the Roman world. Paul didn't endorse it. His letter to Philemon shows that he believed the gospel would eventually transform society from the inside out, breaking down the barriers between slave and free. But in the meantime, Christian slaves lived in a world where their behavior reflected on the gospel. If they were disrespectful or rebellious, unbelievers would use that as an excuse to dismiss

Christianity. Paul wanted slaves to know that even in an unjust situation, their conduct could either advance or hinder the mission of God.

For slaves with Christian masters, the temptation was different. Because they were brothers and sisters in Christ, it might have been easy to become overly casual or disrespectful. "We're equals in God's family, so why should I serve you?" Paul pushes back: "Those who have believing masters must not be disrespectful to them because they are brothers and sisters. Rather, they must serve them all the more." Shared faith doesn't erase earthly responsibilities. It transforms them. Service to a fellow Christian becomes an act of love, not just obligation.

In a remarkable twist, Paul uses a word for the slaves' service that was normally reserved for wealthy benefactors who gave generously to their cities. He's quietly turning the social order upside down. In God's household, the servant who gives faithful labor is the true benefactor.

WHAT THIS MEANS FOR US

First, the church is a family, and families take care of their own. Paul's instructions about widows, elders, and slaves all flow from one big idea: when you belong to God's household, you have obligations to the other members. That means looking out for people who are vulnerable, supporting those who lead faithfully, and refusing to ignore people in need.

Second, family responsibility comes before church responsibility. Before the church steps in to help, Paul expects families to take care of their own. If your grandmother needs help, that's your family's calling first. A community that outsources all its care to institutions while families ignore their own members has missed something essential.

Third, leaders need both support and accountability. It's not enough to pay leaders well and leave them alone. Elders who lead well deserve generous honor, but elders who persist in sin need to be confronted. A church without accountability is a church waiting for disaster.

Fourth, your conduct always represents something bigger than yourself. Whether it was a slave in the first century or a student in a classroom today, the way you behave either draws people toward God or pushes them away. Living with integrity in difficult circumstances is one of the most powerful testimonies you can offer.

TALKING POINTS

1. **Paul tells Timothy to treat older men as fathers, younger men as brothers, older women as mothers, and younger women as sisters.** How would it change the way your church feels if everyone actually practiced this? What would be different?

2. **Paul says that if someone doesn't provide for their own family, they've "denied the faith."** Why do you think he uses such strong language? What does caring for family have to do with faith in God?

3. **Paul instructs the church to support elders who "labor in preaching and teaching."** Why do you think it's important for churches to pay their ministers well? What message does it send when a church doesn't?

4. **Paul tells Timothy to handle accusations against elders carefully, requiring two or three witnesses.** Why do you think he sets this standard? What could go wrong if a leader could be removed based on one person's complaint?

5. **Paul tells slaves to serve respectfully "so that the name of God and the teaching may not be blasphemed."** Can you think of a situation in your own life where your behavior, good or bad, could affect what people think about your faith or about God?

Paul has walked Timothy through the practical realities of caring for God's household: the old and young, widows and elders, masters and slaves. But he has one more thing to say before he closes this letter, and it's about a danger that can destroy any church, any leader, and any life. It's the danger of loving money more than God.

Turn the page.

6

THE CHRIST-SHAPED LIFE

William Makepeace Thackeray's novel *Vanity Fair* follows a young woman named Becky Sharp who has one goal in life: to get rich. Becky is clever, charming, and ruthless. She grows up poor, and she hates it. From the moment she leaves school, every relationship she forms, every friendship she cultivates, every decision she makes is calculated to move her one step closer to wealth and social status. She flatters people she despises. She manipulates people who trust her. She lies without flinching. And for a while, it works. Becky climbs the social ladder, marries into money, and gets a taste of the life she's always wanted.

But none of it lasts. Her schemes unravel. Her marriage collapses. Friends discover who she really is and abandon her. By the end of the story, Becky has gained and lost everything, and the reader is left wondering whether she ever enjoyed a single moment of the life she fought so hard to build. Thackeray titled his novel after a famous marketplace in an older story, a place where everything in the world is for sale: houses, honors, kingdoms, pleasures, lives. The point is simple and devastating. When you spend your whole life chasing money and status, you end up with nothing that matters.

Paul closes his first letter to Timothy with the same warning, and he doesn't hold back. The love of money, he says, is "a root of all kinds of evil." Some people, in their eagerness to get rich, "have wandered away from the faith and pierced themselves with many griefs." If that sounds dramatic, it's because Paul has watched it happen. He has seen teachers in the church twist the gospel into a money-making scheme. He has seen believers abandon everything they once believed because money promised them something the gospel didn't seem to offer. And he wants Timothy to know, in the strongest possible terms, that the Christ-shaped life looks nothing like this.

Paul opens this final section by returning one more time to the false teachers. They teach "a different doctrine" that doesn't agree with "the sound words of our Lord Jesus Christ" or with "the teaching that accords with godliness." Their problem isn't just intellectual error. It's character. Paul says they are "puffed up with conceit" and have "an unhealthy craving for controversy and for quarrels about words."

Look at the results of their teaching: "envy, dissension, slander, evil suspicions, and constant friction." Everything they produce is the opposite of love. Their teaching doesn't build the church up. It tears it apart. And underneath all the arguing and speculation, Paul exposes their real motivation: they imagine "that godliness is a means of gain." They're using the church to make money.

This is the darkest version of false teaching. It's not just wrong ideas. It's exploitation. These teachers have figured out that religious people will pay for spiritual experiences, and they've turned the gospel into a product. The ancient world was full of traveling teachers who charged fees for their wisdom. Some of the false teachers in Ephesus appear to have been doing the same thing, packaging their myths and speculations as premium spiritual knowledge and profiting from people's hunger for God.

GODLINESS WITH CONTENTMENT

Paul's response is one of the most quotable lines in the entire Bible: "There is great gain in godliness, but only when combined with contentment."

The false teachers said godliness was a means of financial gain. Paul turns the phrase on its head. Yes, godliness produces great gain, but not the kind you deposit in a bank. The real gain is contentment: the deep, settled satisfaction that comes from knowing God and being at peace with what he provides.

Then Paul drops a truth that hits like a brick: "For we brought nothing into the world, and we cannot take anything out of the world." Every dollar you earn, every possession you accumulate, every material thing you build your life around stays behind when you die. You arrived with nothing. You'll leave with nothing. Knowing that should change how you think about everything in between.

"But if we have food and clothing, with these we will be content." Paul isn't saying Christians should aim for poverty. He's saying that the basics of life—enough to eat and a roof over your head—should be enough to satisfy you. When they are, you're free. Free from the anxiety of always wanting more. Free from the trap of measuring your worth by what you own.

THE TRAP

For those who aren't content, Paul paints a terrifying picture: "Those who desire to be rich fall into temptation, into a snare, into many senseless and harmful desires that plunge people into ruin and destruction."

Notice the language. Fall. Snare. Plunge. Ruin. Destruction. Paul sees the love of money as a downward spiral. It doesn't start with a dramatic decision to abandon God. It starts with a desire, just a small, quiet pull toward wanting more than you need. That desire leads to temptation. Temptation leads to a trap. And once you're trapped, you sink.

Then comes the famous proverb: "For the love of money is a root of all kinds of evil. It is through this craving that some have wandered away from the faith and pierced themselves with many griefs."

Two things to notice. First, the problem isn't money itself. It's the *love* of money. Money is a tool. It can be used for enormous good. But when you start loving it, when it becomes the thing you think about, plan around, and sacrifice for, it becomes an idol. Second, the consequences are personal. People who chase money don't just damage their finances. They damage their faith, their relationships, and their own souls. Paul says they "pierce themselves," as if they're driving nails into their own hearts. Nobody does this to them. They do it to themselves.

THE MAN OF GOD

Paul now turns directly to Timothy with one of the most powerful personal charges in all his letters. "But as for you, O man of God, flee these things."

"Man of God" is a title from the Old Testament, given to Moses, Samuel, Elijah, and David. By using it here, Paul is placing Timothy in the company of the greatest leaders in Israel's history. It's both an honor and a weight. Timothy isn't just a young church worker. He's a man of God, and that identity demands a certain kind of life.

"Pursue righteousness, godliness, faith, love, steadfastness, gentleness." Six virtues. Each one the opposite of what the false teachers produce. Where they pursue money, Timothy pursues righteousness. Where they breed dissension, Timothy pursues love. Where they create friction, Timothy pursues gentleness. The Christ-shaped life is defined not by what you accumulate but by what you become.

"Fight the good fight of the faith. Take hold of the eternal life to which you were called." There it is again, the fighter's language Paul loves. The Christian life is a battle, and Timothy is a soldier. But this fight isn't for territory or treasure. It's for faith. And the prize isn't wealth that fades. It's eternal life, the kind of existence that begins now and stretches beyond the grave.

Paul raises the stakes by calling God and Christ Jesus as witnesses. He reminds Timothy of Christ's own faithfulness: Jesus "made the good confession" before Pontius Pilate, speaking truth even when it cost him his life. Now Timothy must do the same. He must "keep the commandment unstained and free from reproach until the appearing of our Lord Jesus Christ."

THE KING OF KINGS

This mention of Christ's future appearing launches Paul into one of the most breathtaking passages of worship in the entire

New Testament: "Which he will display at the proper time: he who is the blessed and only Sovereign, the King of kings and Lord of lords, who alone has immortality, who dwells in unapproachable light, whom no one has ever seen or can see. To him be honor and eternal dominion. Amen."

Paul piles up titles and descriptions like a man trying to capture the uncapturable. God is the only true Sovereign. He outranks every king who ever lived. He alone possesses immortality. He lives in light so brilliant that no human being can approach it or even look at it. In a world where the Roman emperor claimed to be king of kings and lord of lords, Paul quietly and firmly says: No. That title belongs to someone else.

This doxology isn't decoration. It's the foundation of everything Paul has been saying. If God is this great, this powerful, this eternal, then why would anyone trade allegiance to him for money? Why would anyone chase uncertain riches when the King of the universe is offering eternal life?

INSTRUCTIONS FOR THE RICH

After that burst of praise, Paul adds one final practical instruction for wealthy believers. "As for the rich in this present age, charge them not to be haughty, nor to set their hopes on the uncertainty of riches, but on God, who richly provides us with everything to enjoy."

Paul doesn't condemn wealth. He condemns arrogance and misplaced hope. Rich people are in danger not because money is evil but because money creates an illusion of security. It whispers, "You don't need God. You've got this handled."

Paul says that's a lie. Riches are uncertain. They can vanish overnight. Only God is a reliable foundation.

And what should the rich do with their money? "They are to do good, to be rich in good works, to be generous and ready to share, thus storing up treasure for themselves as a good foundation for the future, so that they may take hold of that which is truly life."

The phrase "truly life" echoes Jesus' own teaching. The real life, the life that matters, isn't measured by your bank account. It's measured by your generosity, your faithfulness, and your trust in the God who gives all good things.

GUARD THE DEPOSIT

Paul closes the letter the way he opened it: with a personal plea to Timothy. "O Timothy, guard the deposit entrusted to you." The "deposit" is the gospel, the body of truth Paul received from Christ and passed down to Timothy. It's not Timothy's to revise, edit, or improve. It's his to protect and proclaim. "Avoid the irreverent babble and contradictions of what is falsely called knowledge," Paul adds, taking one last shot at the false teachers who dress up their empty speculations as wisdom.

"Grace be with you." And with those four words, the letter ends.

WHAT THIS MEANS FOR US

First, contentment is a superpower. The world tells you that happiness is always one purchase away. Paul says the opposite. Real satisfaction comes from knowing God and being at peace with what he provides. Learning to say "I have enough" is one of the most countercultural and freeing things a Christian can do.

Second, the love of money will cost you more than money can buy. Paul warns that chasing wealth leads to a downward spiral of temptation, traps, and self-destruction. That doesn't mean money is bad. It means that making money your goal will wreck your life and your faith. Hold it loosely.

Third, generosity is the antidote to greed. Paul's instruction to the rich isn't "feel guilty." It's "be generous." Use what God has given you to do good, share freely, and store up treasure that lasts forever. The best use of money is giving it away.

Fourth, guard the gospel like your life depends on it, because it does. Paul's final word to Timothy is a charge to protect the truth he's been entrusted with. Every generation faces the temptation to water down, add to, or replace the gospel with something more fashionable. Timothy's job, and ours, is to guard it and pass it on unchanged.

TALKING POINTS

1. **Paul says "the love of money is a root of all kinds of evil."** Do you agree? Can you think of examples from history, from the news, or from your own experience where the love of money caused real damage?

2. **Paul describes contentment as knowing that "if we have food and clothing, we will be content."** Does that sound realistic to you? What makes contentment so hard in a culture that constantly tells you to want more?

3. **Paul tells Timothy to "flee" the love of money and "pursue" righteousness, godliness, faith, love, steadfast-**

ness, and gentleness. Why do you think he uses the words "flee" and "pursue"? What's the difference between just avoiding something bad and actively chasing something good?

4. **Paul instructs the rich to "be generous and ready to share."** If you had a large amount of money, what would you do with it? How would you balance enjoying it and giving it away?

5. **The letter ends with Paul telling Timothy to "guard the deposit."** What does it look like practically for a young person today to guard the gospel? What are some "false knowledge" claims that people your age might encounter?

Paul's first letter to Timothy was about protecting the church: its doctrine, its leaders, its people, and its mission. But Paul isn't done. He has a second letter to write, and this one comes from a very different place. When Paul wrote 1 Timothy, he was free. When he writes 2 Timothy, he's on death row, and he knows the end is near. Everything he says next carries the weight of a man's final words.

Turn the page.

7

FAN THE FLAME

The 1982 animated film *The Secret of NIMH* tells the story of Mrs. Brisby, a timid field mouse whose youngest son is deathly ill. The family's home is about to be destroyed by a farmer's plow, and she has to move her children to safety. But her sick son can't be moved without dying. Mrs. Brisby is small, terrified, and completely out of her depth. She's not a warrior. She's not a leader. She's a quiet, anxious mother who would rather hide from danger than face it.

But she doesn't hide. Step by terrifying step, she pushes past her fear. She ventures into the den of a terrifying owl. She infiltrates the rats' colony beneath the rosebush. She faces creatures and situations that would paralyze anyone, let alone a tiny mouse who has never done anything brave in her life. And what drives her forward isn't confidence in her own strength. It's love for her children and a refusal to let fear have the last word.

Paul's second letter to Timothy reads like a message written to someone who might be tempted to hide. Timothy was young, possibly timid by nature, and facing a storm of opposition. Nearly everyone who should have stood with Paul had abandoned him. False teachers were gaining ground. And now Paul was writing from a Roman prison cell, probably chained to a guard, knowing that execution was likely. If there was ever a moment when fear might have paralyzed Timothy into silence, this was it.

But Paul's message is the opposite of what fear would expect: don't shrink back. Fan the flame. The Spirit God gave you isn't a spirit of fear. It's a spirit of power, love, and self-control.

A LETTER FROM DEATH ROW

Before we get into the content, you need to feel the weight of this letter. When Paul wrote 1 Timothy, he was a free man, traveling and ministering. When he writes 2 Timothy, everything has changed. He's in prison in Rome. His friends have scattered. He's cold (he'll later ask Timothy to bring his cloak). He expects to die. This is Paul's final letter, his last will and testament, the words he chose to leave behind for the person he trusted most in the world.

That changes how you read every sentence. This isn't casual instruction. This is a dying man telling his spiritual son what matters most.

Paul opens with his usual greeting, calling Timothy "my beloved child" and wishing him "grace, mercy, and peace from God the Father and Christ Jesus our Lord." But immediately the tone becomes deeply personal. "I remember you constantly in my prayers night and day. As I remember your tears, I long to see you, that I may be filled with joy."

Picture that. Paul, alone in a dungeon, praying for Timothy and remembering the last time they were together, when

Timothy wept at their parting. Even in chains, Paul's thoughts aren't about himself. They're about his son in the faith.

A HERITAGE OF FAITH

Paul then does something beautiful. He reminds Timothy of where his faith came from. "I am reminded of your sincere faith, a faith that dwelt first in your grandmother Lois and your mother Eunice and now, I am sure, dwells in you as well."

Three generations of faith: grandmother, mother, son. Lois believed. She passed her faith to Eunice. Eunice passed it to Timothy. Long before Paul ever met him, Timothy had been shaped by the prayers and teaching of two faithful women. They had taught him the Scriptures from childhood. They had shown him what trust in God looked like in daily life. And that foundation held.

Paul wants Timothy to remember this because the faith Timothy carries is not something he invented. It's a living inheritance, passed from one generation to the next, stretching all the way back through Israel's history to Abraham himself. Paul says he serves God "as did my ancestors, with a clear conscience." The God Timothy trusts is the same God Paul's Jewish forefathers worshiped. The faith is ancient. It is tested. And it is alive in Timothy right now.

STIR UP THE GIFT

"For this reason I remind you to fan into flame the gift of God, which is in you through the laying on of my hands." Somewhere earlier in Timothy's ministry, Paul had laid hands on him in a moment of commissioning. At that moment, God gave Timothy a spiritual gift for his work, an empowerment by the Holy Spirit for the ministry he was called to do. Paul doesn't specify exactly what the gift was, but it was connected to Timothy's calling as a teacher, leader, and guardian of the gospel.

Now Paul says: fan it into flame. The image is vivid. A fire that isn't tended will die down to embers. It doesn't go out all at once. It fades. It cools. It becomes less and less until there's nothing left but ash. Paul is telling Timothy that spiritual gifts work the same way. If you don't use them, they weaken. If you don't exercise your calling, it atrophies. Timothy can't afford to coast. He has to actively, intentionally stir up the fire God placed inside him.

Why might Timothy have been tempted to let the fire die? Because of fear. Paul addresses it directly: "For God gave us a spirit not of fear but of power and love and self-control."

This is one of those verses that deserves to be memorized. Whatever Timothy was facing, whether it was the fear of persecution, the intimidation of older critics, or the sheer weight of responsibility, Paul reminds him that fear doesn't come from God. What God gives is power (the strength to do what needs to be done), love (the motivation that makes courage possible), and self-control (the discipline to stay steady when everything feels chaotic).

Mrs. Brisby didn't fight the owl because she was naturally brave. She fought because love was stronger than fear. Timothy doesn't need to be naturally bold. He needs to rely on the Spirit who is already at work inside him.

DO NOT BE ASHAMED

Paul gets to the heart of the chapter: "Therefore do not be ashamed of the testimony about our Lord, nor of me his prisoner, but share in suffering for the gospel by the power of God."

There are three things Timothy might be tempted to feel ashamed of. First, the gospel itself. In a world that worshiped power, success, and status, the message of a crucified Savior sounded like foolishness. Second, Paul. His mentor was a prisoner, chained like a criminal. Associating with Paul meant associating with shame. Third, suffering. Following the gospel doesn't lead to comfort and popularity. It leads to hardship.

Paul doesn't sugarcoat this. He tells Timothy to "share in suffering." Not avoid it. Not work around it. Share in it. But he also tells him the source of his strength: "by the power of God." Timothy doesn't suffer alone, and he doesn't suffer in his own strength.

THE GOSPEL IN A SINGLE BREATH

Paul then gives one of the most concentrated summaries of the gospel in all his letters: "God saved us and called us to a holy calling, not because of our works but because of his own purpose and grace, which he gave us in Christ Jesus before the ages began, and which now has been manifested through the appearing of our Savior Christ Jesus, who abolished death and brought life and immortality to light through the gospel."

Read that slowly. Every phrase matters.

God *saved* us. Salvation is God's work from start to finish. He *called* us to a holy calling. Being saved isn't just about escaping punishment. It's about being set apart for a new kind of life. *Not because of our works* but because of *his own purpose and grace.* We didn't earn it. We can't earn it. God decided to save us before we ever existed, "before the ages began." And this plan was revealed "through the appearing of our Savior Christ Jesus," who did the unthinkable: he "abolished death and brought life and immortality to light."

Death abolished. Life revealed. That's the gospel. And it's the reason Paul can sit in a Roman prison, facing execution, and write without despair. Death has already been defeated. The worst thing the empire can do to him is send him home.

"For this gospel I was appointed a herald and an apostle and a teacher, which is why I suffer as I do. But I am not ashamed, for I know whom I have believed, and I am convinced that he is able to guard until that day what has been entrusted to me."

Paul doesn't say "I know *what* I have believed." He says "I know *whom* I have believed." His confidence isn't in a set of doctrines, though the doctrines matter. His confidence is in a person: Jesus Christ, who is powerful enough to protect the gospel and everyone who carries it, all the way to the end.

GUARD THE DEPOSIT

Paul now hands the responsibility to Timothy. "Follow the pattern of the sound words that you have heard from me, in the faith and love that are in Christ Jesus. By the Holy Spirit who dwells within us, guard the good deposit entrusted to you."

The "deposit" is the gospel itself. Paul received it from Christ. He passed it to Timothy. Now Timothy must protect it, not by locking it away but by teaching it faithfully, living it consistently, and defending it from corruption. And he doesn't have to do this alone. The Holy Spirit, who dwells inside every Christian, is the ultimate guardian of the truth.

THOSE WHO STAYED AND THOSE WHO LEFT

Paul closes the chapter with two contrasting examples. "You are aware that all who are in Asia turned away from me, among whom are Phygelus and Hermogenes." Nearly everyone had abandoned Paul. When he was arrested, the Christians of Asia Minor apparently decided the cost of association was too high. Two men, Phygelus and Hermogenes, are named as leaders in this desertion. We know nothing else about them. Their names survive only because they walked away.

But then there was Onesiphorus. "May the Lord grant mercy to the household of Onesiphorus, for he often refreshed me and was not ashamed of my chains. On the contrary, when he arrived in Rome, he searched for me earnestly and found me."

While everyone else ran, Onesiphorus came looking. He traveled to Rome, searched through the city's prisons, and tracked Paul down. He wasn't ashamed of Paul's chains. He refreshed him, probably with food, companionship, and encouragement. Paul prays that God will show mercy to Onesiphorus and his family, because this one man's loyalty shone like a light in the darkness.

The contrast is deliberate. Timothy has a choice. He can follow the crowd and walk away, or he can follow Onesiphorus and walk toward the suffering. Paul trusts him to choose well.

WHAT THIS MEANS FOR US

First, your spiritual heritage matters. Timothy's faith was built on the foundation laid by his grandmother and mother. If you've been blessed with parents or grandparents who taught you about God, don't take that for granted. And if you haven't, know that God can still reach you. Paul himself came to faith through a dramatic encounter with Jesus, not a family tradition. Either way, the faith you receive is meant to be passed on.

Second, spiritual gifts must be fanned into flame. God gives gifts, but he expects you to use them. A talent that goes unpracticed, a calling that goes unfollowed, a fire that goes untended will all eventually fade. Whatever God has placed inside you, stir it up. Use it. Develop it. Don't let fear or laziness turn a flame into an ember.

Third, the Spirit God gave you is not a spirit of fear. Fear is real. It's powerful. But it's not from God. When you feel paralyzed by the thought of standing up for your faith, speaking the truth, or doing something hard for God, remember: you have been given power, love, and self-control. Those three things are more than enough to face anything.

Fourth, the gospel is worth suffering for. Paul didn't pretend that following Jesus was easy. He told Timothy straight: you will suffer. But he also showed him that suffering for the gospel is not pointless. It's participation in the mission of a God who abolished death and promised eternal life. That changes everything.

TALKING POINTS

1. **Paul reminds Timothy of the faith of his grandmother Lois and his mother Eunice.** Who are the people in your life who have most shaped your faith? What did they do that made such an impact?

2. **Paul says God gave us "a spirit not of fear but of power and love and self-control."** Which of those three do you think you need most right now? Why?

3. **Paul tells Timothy not to be ashamed of the gospel or of Paul the prisoner.** Have you ever felt embarrassed or afraid to be associated with your faith? What happened?

4. **Almost everyone in Asia abandoned Paul, but Onesiphorus searched for him and found him.** What do you think made the difference between those who left and the one who stayed? What can you learn from Onesiphorus' example?

5. **Paul says, "I know whom I have believed, and I am convinced that he is able to guard what has been entrusted to me."** What do you think is the difference between knowing *what* you believe and knowing *whom* you believe? Why does that distinction matter?

Paul has reminded Timothy of his heritage, his gift, and the gospel that's worth everything. But the work ahead is hard, and Timothy will need more than just encouragement. He'll need endurance. Paul is about to give him three pictures of what that looks like: a soldier, an athlete, and a farmer.

Turn the page.

8

A GOOD SOLDIER

Almost two thousand years ago, a Roman emperor named Marcus Aurelius sat in a military tent on the cold frontier of the empire and wrote a private journal. He wasn't writing for an audience. He was writing to himself. And what he wrote, later published as *The Meditations*, is one of the most honest books about discipline and endurance ever put on paper.

Marcus Aurelius didn't write about how great it was to be emperor. He wrote about how hard it was to do the right thing. He reminded himself to wake up early even when he didn't feel like it. He told himself to stop complaining about difficult people. He urged himself to stay focused on his duty instead of chasing comfort. "At dawn, when you have trouble getting out of bed," he wrote, "tell yourself: I have to go to work, as a human being." He was emperor of the most powerful nation on earth, and he still had to give himself a pep talk every morning.

Paul wasn't an emperor. He was a prisoner. But in 2 Timothy 2 he does something strikingly similar. He sits in a Roman cell and writes to Timothy about what it takes to endure, to keep going when everything in you wants to stop. And he does it with three images that would have been immediately recognizable to anyone in the ancient world: a soldier, an athlete, and a farmer.

Each one teaches the same lesson from a different angle. There are no shortcuts in the Christian life. Faithfulness is built through discipline, endurance, and sweat.

BE STRONG IN GRACE

Paul opens the chapter with a command that sounds impossible: "You then, my child, be strengthened by the grace that is in Christ Jesus."

"You then" is deliberate. In the previous chapter, Paul had just told Timothy about all the people who abandoned him. Nearly everyone in Asia had walked away. The pressure on Timothy to do the same must have been enormous. But Paul says: "You, Timothy, be different. Be strong."

Not strong in yourself. Strong in grace. Paul isn't telling a timid man to suddenly become fearless through willpower. He's telling him to draw his strength from a source outside himself: the grace of Jesus Christ. This is the same grace that saved Paul the persecutor, the same grace that sustains Paul the prisoner. And it's available to Timothy too.

Then comes the practical instruction: "What you have heard from me in the presence of many witnesses, entrust to faithful men, who will be able to teach others also."

This single verse contains four generations of gospel transmission. Christ entrusted the truth to Paul. Paul passed it to Timothy. Timothy is to pass it to faithful people. And those faithful people will teach still others. The chain must not break. This is the true apostolic succession: not a line of titles or offices, but a living chain of people who receive the truth and pass it on unchanged.

THREE PICTURES OF ENDURANCE

Paul now paints three vivid pictures to show Timothy what this kind of faithfulness looks like in practice.

The Soldier. "Share in suffering as a good soldier of Christ Jesus. No soldier gets entangled in civilian pursuits, since his aim is to please the one who enlisted him."

A soldier on active duty has one job: serve his commanding officer. He doesn't get distracted by side projects or hobbies. He doesn't start a business on the side while he's supposed to be at his post. He accepts hardship as part of the deal. Cold, hunger, danger, exhaustion: these aren't interruptions to a soldier's life. They *are* the soldier's life. And a good soldier endures them without complaint because he has a mission that matters more than his comfort.

Paul isn't saying Christians should abandon normal life. He's saying that nothing should pull you away from your primary calling. If you belong to Christ, your first loyalty is to him. Everything else is secondary.

The Athlete. "An athlete is not crowned unless he competes according to the rules."

In the Greek and Roman games, athletes trained for months. They followed strict diets. They submitted to brutal practice schedules. And when competition day came, they had to follow the rules of the event. If you cheated, cut corners, or broke the rules, you were disqualified. No matter how fast you ran, you didn't get the crown.

The Christian life has rules too. Not rules that earn salvation (Paul has already made clear that salvation is a gift of grace), but standards of faithfulness and obedience that mark a life truly lived for God. You can't just do whatever you want and expect God's approval. The way you run matters as much as whether you run.

The Farmer. "It is the hardworking farmer who ought to have the first share of the crops."

Farming is unglamorous. There's no crowd cheering while you plow a field. Nobody hands you a trophy for pulling weeds. But the farmer who shows up every day, who puts in the work season after season, who endures drought and insects and back-breaking labor, is the one who eventually sees the harvest. And Paul says that farmer deserves the first share of what he's produced.

Spiritual fruit works the same way. Love, patience, faithfulness, the growth of new Christians: none of these happen overnight. They're the result of long, steady, often unnoticed labor. The Christian who toils faithfully in teaching, in prayer, in service, and in relationship will eventually see a harvest.

Paul wraps up the three metaphors with an invitation: "Think over what I say, for the Lord will give you understanding in everything." In other words, don't just read these images and move on. Sit with them. Chew on them. Let the Lord show you how they apply to your specific situation.

REMEMBER JESUS CHRIST

Paul now grounds everything in the person at the center of it all: "Remember Jesus Christ, risen from the dead, the offspring of David, as preached in my gospel, for which I am suffering, bound with chains as a criminal. But the word of God is not bound!"

Paul is in chains. But the gospel isn't. They can lock up the messenger, but they can't lock up the message. This is one of the most defiant statements in the entire New Testament. The Roman Empire, with all its power, could imprison Paul. It could not imprison the truth.

And the truth Paul proclaims is simple: Jesus Christ, a real descendant of David, was raised from the dead. That's the gospel in one sentence. The resurrection is the proof that everything Jesus said was true, that death has been defeated, and that eternal life is real.

Paul endures everything, even chains, "for the sake of the elect, that they also may obtain the salvation that is in Christ Jesus with eternal glory." He's not suffering for himself. He's suffering so that others can hear the gospel and be saved.

A TRUSTWORTHY SAYING

Paul then quotes what appears to be an early Christian hymn, and it's one of the most powerful passages in the letter: "If we have died with him, we will also live with him; if we endure, we will also reign with him; if we deny him, he also will deny us; if we are faithless, he remains faithful, for he cannot deny himself."

Four lines. Four truths.

The first two are promises. If you die to yourself and follow Christ, you will live forever with him. If you endure suffering and hardship, you will reign with him in glory. The road to life goes through death. The road to glory goes through endurance.

The last two are warnings. If you deny Christ, he will deny you. This echoes Jesus' own words: "Whoever denies me before men, I also will deny before my Father who is in heaven." And if you are faithless, God remains faithful, but faithful to *what*? Faithful to his own character, which means faithful to both his promises and his warnings. God will not change his standards to accommodate our unfaithfulness. He cannot deny himself.

THE APPROVED WORKER

Paul shifts to a new set of images for the second half of the chapter. "Do your best to present yourself to God as one approved, a worker who has no need to be ashamed, rightly handling the word of truth."

"Rightly handling" translates a word that means to cut straight. A good worker cuts a straight line. A carpenter, a stonemason, a tailor: each one is measured by how precisely they handle their material. Timothy's material is the word of truth, the gospel. He must handle it with care and precision, not twisting it, not adding to it, not neglecting parts of it.

By contrast, Hymenaeus and Philetus are examples of bad workers. Paul says they "have swerved from the truth, saying that the resurrection has already taken place." They were teaching that the future resurrection had already happened, probably meaning that the only "resurrection" is a spiritual experience in this life. By saying this, they were "upsetting the faith of some." Bad teaching has real casualties.

But Paul reassures Timothy: "God's firm foundation stands, bearing this seal: 'The Lord knows those who are his,' and, 'Let everyone who names the name of the Lord depart from iniquity.'" No matter how many people swerve from the truth, God's foundation doesn't move. He knows who belongs to him, and he expects them to live accordingly.

VESSELS AND SERVANTS

Paul uses one more image: a great house with different kinds of containers. Some are gold and silver, for honorable use. Others are wood and clay, for common or dishonorable purposes. "If anyone cleanses himself from what is dishonorable, he will be a vessel for honorable use, set apart as holy, useful to the master of the house, ready for every good work."

The point is clear. You choose what kind of vessel you are by how you live. Cleanse yourself from sin, from the influence of false teaching, from the contamination of bad character, and God will use you for great things.

Paul then gives Timothy the familiar dual command: "Flee youthful passions and pursue righteousness, faith, love, and peace, along with those who call on the Lord from a pure heart." Run from what destroys you. Run toward what builds you. And don't do it alone. Find others who are pursuing the same things.

The chapter closes with a portrait of "the Lord's servant." He must not be quarrelsome but "kind to everyone, able to teach, patiently enduring evil, correcting his opponents with gentleness." Why gentleness? Because the goal isn't to win arguments. The goal is to win people. "God may perhaps grant them repentance leading to a knowledge of the truth, and they may come to their senses and escape from the snare of the devil."

Even the false teachers aren't beyond redemption. They're trapped by the devil, and the Lord's servant approaches them not with rage but with hope.

WHAT THIS MEANS FOR US

First, faithfulness is built through discipline, not inspiration. Soldiers train. Athletes follow rules. Farmers work the soil day after day. None of them succeed by waiting for the right feeling to show up. If you want to be faithful to God over the long haul, build habits now: reading Scripture, praying, serving, and staying connected to other believers.

Second, the gospel must be passed on. Paul gave it to Timothy. Timothy must give it to faithful people. Those people must teach others. You're part of that chain. What you learn about Jesus, you're responsible to share.

Third, how you handle truth matters. There's a difference between cutting straight and cutting crooked. You can twist the Bible to say almost anything if you try hard enough. But the approved worker handles God's word with honesty, precision, and humility. That means studying it carefully, not just picking verses that support what you already want to believe.

Fourth, gentleness is strength, not weakness. The Lord's servant corrects opponents not with anger or contempt but with patience and kindness. Why? Because even people who are trapped in error might be rescued. Gentleness leaves the door open for God to work.

TALKING POINTS

1. **Paul uses three metaphors: a soldier, an athlete, and a farmer.** Which one do you connect with most? Why? What does that image teach you about following Jesus?

2. **Paul says the word of God "is not bound," even though Paul himself is in chains.** Can you think of examples from history or today where attempts to silence the gospel actually caused it to spread further?

3. **The hymn in verses 11–13 includes both promises and warnings.** Why do you think Paul includes both? How should the warning "if we deny him, he also will deny us" affect how we live?

4. **Paul tells Timothy to "flee youthful passions and pursue righteousness, faith, love, and peace."** What "youthful passions" do you think are the biggest threats to people your age? What does it look like practically to run from those and run toward something better?

5. **Paul says the Lord's servant should correct opponents "with gentleness."** Why is this so hard to do? Can you think of a time when someone corrected you gently, and it actually made you want to change?

Paul has given Timothy everything he needs: the metaphors of endurance, the model of Christ, the hymn of promise and warning, and the portrait of the approved worker. But the road ahead is going to get darker. Paul has seen the future, and he has something urgent to say about what the last days will look like and where Timothy will find the strength to survive them.

Turn the page.

9

EVERYTHING YOU NEED

The Goonies is a 1985 adventure film about a group of kids from a working-class neighborhood called the Goon Docks. Their families are about to lose their homes to developers, and the kids have one last weekend before everything changes. Then Mikey Walsh finds something in his attic: an old treasure map that supposedly leads to the lost fortune of a legendary pirate named One-Eyed Willy.

What follows is one of the wildest treasure hunts ever put on screen. The kids follow the map through underground tunnels, past deadly booby traps, and around every obstacle the pirate left behind to protect his gold. The map is everything. Without it, they'd walk straight into traps. Without it, they'd take wrong turns and dead ends. Without it, they'd never reach the treasure. Every time they're lost or scared or ready to give up, they go back to the map. It tells them where they are, what to watch out for, and where they need to go next.

Paul's message to Timothy in 2 Timothy 3 works on a similar logic. The world around Timothy is full of traps. False teachers are everywhere. People are being deceived. The moral landscape is collapsing. And into this chaos, Paul points Timothy to the one thing that will guide him through it all: the Scriptures. "All Scripture is breathed out by God," Paul writes, "and profitable for teaching, for reproof, for correction, and for training in righteousness, so that the man of God may be complete, equipped for every good work."

The Scriptures are the map. They tell you where the traps are. They show you the right path. And they lead you to the treasure that actually matters: salvation through faith in Christ Jesus.

THE DARK FORECAST

Paul opens the chapter with a blunt warning: "Understand this, that in the last days there will come times of difficulty." We've already seen that "the last days" in the New Testament don't refer only to some far-off future. The last days began when Jesus came. We're living in them right now. Paul isn't describing a world Timothy won't live to see. He's describing the world Timothy is already living in, and the world we live in too. There will be seasons of unusual danger and hardship, and Timothy needs to understand why.

The reason? People. Paul launches into one of the longest vice lists in his letters. "People will be lovers of self, lovers of money, proud, arrogant, abusive, disobedient to their parents, ungrateful, unholy, heartless, unappeasable, slanderous, without self-control, brutal, not loving good, treacherous, reckless, swollen with conceit, lovers of pleasure rather than lovers of God."

That's nineteen descriptions, and they're devastating. Notice how it starts and ends. It begins with "lovers of self" and ends with "lovers of pleasure rather than lovers of God." The whole list is a portrait of what happens when people put themselves at the center of the universe instead of God. When you love yourself above everything, you become proud. When you're proud, you become arrogant. When you're arrogant, you treat others with contempt. And the spiral goes downward from there: disobedience, ingratitude, cruelty, betrayal, recklessness.

But here's the most disturbing part. These aren't just descriptions of people outside the church. Paul says these people have "the appearance of godliness, but deny its power." They show up on Sunday morning looking religious. They know the right words. They go through the motions. But their lives tell a completely different story. Their religion is a mask, not a reality.

Paul's instruction to Timothy is direct: "Avoid such people."

CREEPING INTO HOUSEHOLDS

Paul gets more specific. "For among them are those who creep into households and capture weak-willed people, burdened with sins and led astray by various passions, always learning and never able to arrive at a knowledge of the truth."

The false teachers aren't standing on street corners announcing their intentions. They're slipping in through the back door, working their way into people's homes and lives, targeting those who are most vulnerable. These victims are described as "always learning and never able to arrive at a knowledge of the truth." They're spiritually curious but spiritually rootless, always chasing the next exciting idea but never settling on the truth.

Paul compares these false teachers to Jannes and Jambres, the Egyptian magicians who opposed Moses in the court of

Pharaoh. According to Jewish tradition, those were the names of the sorcerers who tried to imitate God's miracles during the plagues of Egypt. They could produce a counterfeit version of some of the signs, but they couldn't match the real thing. Eventually their tricks failed, and the truth won.

Paul says the false teachers in Timothy's day are the same: "They oppose the truth, men corrupted in mind and disqualified regarding the faith. But they will not get very far, for their folly will be plain to all, as was that of those two."

That's an encouraging promise. Falsehood has a shelf life. It looks impressive for a while, but eventually it collapses under its own weight. The truth, by contrast, endures.

BUT AS FOR YOU

Twice in this chapter Paul uses the phrase "But as for you" to draw a sharp line between Timothy and the people he's just described. It's the same move Paul has made throughout this letter: everyone else may be drifting, but Timothy must stand firm.

The first time (verse 10), Paul reminds Timothy of what he's already been doing: "You, however, have followed my teaching, my conduct, my aim in life, my faith, my patience, my love, my steadfastness, my persecutions and sufferings."

Nine things Timothy had observed and imitated in Paul's life. Not just his teaching, but his whole way of living. Timothy had watched Paul up close for years, through good times and terrible ones. He knew what Paul taught. He knew how Paul lived. He knew what drove Paul forward. And he knew what Paul had suffered.

Paul specifically mentions the persecutions he endured in Antioch, Iconium, and Lystra, cities Timothy knew well since he grew up in that region. In Lystra, Paul had been stoned by a mob and left for dead outside the city walls. Timothy may have witnessed this as a boy. And yet, Paul writes, "The Lord rescued me from them all."

Then comes a verse every Christian needs to hear: "Indeed, all who desire to live a godly life in Christ Jesus will be persecuted." That's not a possibility. It's a promise. If you're serious about following Jesus, you will face opposition. Not because you did something wrong, but because the world pushes back against godliness. The false teachers won't be persecuted because they've blended in with the world. Timothy will be persecuted because he hasn't.

Meanwhile, "evil people and impostors will go on from bad to worse, deceiving and being deceived." The false teachers aren't just lying to others. They're lying to themselves. They've become trapped in their own deception.

CONTINUE IN WHAT YOU HAVE LEARNED

The second "But as for you" (verse 14) is the heart of the chapter: "But as for you, continue in what you have learned and have firmly believed, knowing from whom you learned it."

In a world of constant change and relentless pressure to adopt the latest ideas, Paul's command is breathtakingly simple: don't move. Stay where you are. Continue in the truth you've already received. Not because there's nothing new to learn, but because the foundation doesn't change. The gospel Timothy received from Paul, and the Scriptures Timothy learned from his grandmother and mother as a child, are the same truth that will carry him through every storm.

Paul gives two reasons Timothy can trust this truth. First, he knows who taught it to him. Timothy's teachers weren't random strangers. They were Paul the apostle, who received his message from Christ himself, and Lois and Eunice, whose sincere faith shaped Timothy from infancy. The character of the teacher confirms the quality of the teaching.

Second, Timothy has known "the sacred writings" since childhood, and those Scriptures "are able to make you wise for salvation through faith in Christ Jesus." The Old Testament that Timothy's mother and grandmother taught him from the time he could listen wasn't just ancient history. It was the story of God's rescue plan, pointing forward to Jesus the Messiah. And when you read it through the lens of faith in Christ, everything comes into focus.

THE GOD-BREATHED BOOK

This brings us to one of the most important verses in the entire Bible:

"All Scripture is breathed out by God and profitable for teaching, for reproof, for correction, and for training in righteousness, so that the man of God may be complete, equipped for every good work."

"All Scripture." Not some of it. Not just the parts you like. All of it. Both the Old Testament and the New.

"Breathed out by God." Scripture didn't originate in the minds of clever human authors. It came from God himself. The image is of God's breath carrying his words into existence, just as his breath brought creation into being in Genesis. The human authors were real people who wrote in their own styles and from their own experiences, but the ultimate source of what they wrote was God.

And because Scripture comes from God, it is "profitable" in four specific ways. Teaching gives you the truth. Reproof shows you where you've gone wrong. Correction sets you back on the right path. And training in righteousness builds the habits and character of a godly life. Together, these four functions cover everything. Scripture diagnoses the problem and provides the cure. It shows you the standard and trains you to meet it.

The result? The person who lives by Scripture will be "complete, equipped for every good work." Not lacking anything essential. Not missing any tool needed for the job. Complete.

This is Paul's ultimate answer to every threat Timothy faces. False teachers? Scripture exposes them. Moral chaos? Scripture provides the standard. Confusion about the gospel? Scripture makes you wise for salvation. Fear of the future? Scripture trains you for whatever comes. You don't need a new revelation. You don't need a trendy philosophy. You need the old, living, God-breathed word.

WHAT THIS MEANS FOR US

First, difficult times are normal, not exceptional. Paul says the last days include "times of difficulty." If you're surprised by opposition, hostility, or moral confusion in the world around you, you shouldn't be. This is exactly what Paul predicted. The question isn't whether trouble will come. It's whether you'll be ready when it does.

Second, religious appearances can be deceiving. Some of the most dangerous people Paul describes have "the appearance of godliness." Just because someone uses spiritual language, attends church, or carries a Bible doesn't mean they're trustworthy. The test is always whether their life matches their words and whether their teaching lines up with the gospel.

Third, who teaches you matters. Paul tells Timothy to remember "from whom" he learned the truth. Surround yourself with people whose faith is genuine, whose character is consistent, and whose teaching comes from Scripture. The right mentors can anchor your faith for a lifetime.

Fourth, Scripture is everything you need. It's God-breathed. It teaches, corrects, and trains. It makes you wise for salvation. It equips you for every good work. In a world full of competing voices and shifting opinions, the Bible is the one source you can trust completely, because it comes from the one God who never lies.

TALKING POINTS

1. **Paul's vice list in verses 2–5 starts with "lovers of self" and ends with "lovers of pleasure rather than lovers of God."** Why do you think self-love is at the root of so many other problems? What does it look like when someone truly loves God more than themselves?

2. **Paul says the false teachers had "the appearance of godliness but denied its power."** What do you think the "power" of godliness actually is? How can you tell the difference between real faith and fake religion?

3. **Paul writes that "all who desire to live a godly life in Christ Jesus will be persecuted."** Does that match your experience? What kinds of persecution do Christians face today, even if it looks different from what Paul experienced?

4. **Paul says Scripture is "profitable for teaching, for reproof, for correction, and for training in righteousness."** Which of these four purposes do you think is hardest to accept? Why is it difficult to let the Bible not only teach you but also correct you?

5. **Paul tells Timothy to "continue in what you have learned."** In a world that's always telling you to move on to the next new thing, what does it look like to be rooted and stable in your faith without being rigid or closed-minded?

Timothy has the map. He has the Scriptures, the example of Paul, and the heritage of faithful teachers stretching back to his childhood. But Paul has one more charge to deliver, and it may be the most urgent words he ever wrote. He's about to look Timothy in the eye, with God and Christ Jesus as his witnesses, and give him a final command that will echo across the centuries.

Turn the page.

10

PREACH THE WORD

James Fenimore Cooper's novel *The Last of the Mohicans* is set during the French and Indian War in the 1750s. At the center of the story is a man named Chingachgook, the last surviving chief of the Mohican people. His world is vanishing. The forests he grew up in are being swallowed by war. His people are gone. His son, Uncas, the last young warrior who could carry the Mohican name into the future, is killed in the novel's final battle. When the story ends, Chingachgook stands alone, the last of his line, with nothing left but the legacy of who his people were and what they stood for.

There's a moment near the end of the book where a wise elder says of Chingachgook's people that they were brave, faithful, and true. The Mohicans are gone, but their character endures in the memory of everyone who knew them. The story isn't really about defeat. It's about what remains when a life of courage and faithfulness reaches its end.

That's the atmosphere of 2 Timothy 4. Paul is writing what he knows are likely his final words. He's in a Roman prison, abandoned by most of his friends, awaiting execution. His long race is nearly over. And like Chingachgook standing at the end of his story, Paul doesn't collapse into despair. Instead, he looks backward with gratitude, forward with confidence, and straight at Timothy with one last, burning command: preach the word. Don't stop. Don't quit. Don't let what I've given my life for die with me.

These are the last recorded words of the apostle Paul. They deserve to be read slowly.

THE MOST SOLEMN CHARGE

Paul opens with a declaration so weighty it practically shakes the page: "I charge you in the presence of God and of Christ Jesus, who is to judge the living and the dead, and by his appearing and his kingdom: preach the word."

Think about what Paul is doing here. He's calling God and Christ Jesus as witnesses to his command. He's invoking the coming judgment, when every person who ever lived will stand before Christ. He's pointing to the future kingdom that Christ will establish when he returns. And in the presence of all that eternal reality, Paul issues a charge that's only three words long: preach the word.

Not "preach your opinions." Not "preach what people want to hear." Preach the word. The same deposit of truth that Paul received from Christ, entrusted to Timothy, and commanded him to pass on to faithful people. That word—the gospel, the Scriptures, the sound teaching—is what Timothy must proclaim.

Paul then tells him how to do it. "Be ready in season and out of season." Whether the timing feels right or not, whether people are eager to listen or resistant, Timothy must be ready to speak. "Reprove, rebuke, and exhort, with complete patience and teaching." Sometimes the word will need to confront sin. Sometimes it will need to correct error. Sometimes it will need to encourage the discouraged. But always, in every situation, Timothy must be patient and thorough, never rushing through the truth or dumbing it down.

WHY URGENCY MATTERS

Paul explains why this charge is so urgent: "The time is coming when people will not endure sound teaching, but having itching ears they will accumulate for themselves teachers to suit their own passions, and will turn away from listening to the truth and wander into myths."

"Itching ears" is one of the most vivid phrases Paul ever coined. Imagine an itch you can't stop scratching. These are people who want to hear something that feels good, something that confirms what they already want to believe. Instead of listening to truth that challenges them, they shop around for teachers who tell them what they want to hear. They replace the gospel with myths, trading solid food for candy.

Paul has seen this coming for years. The false teachers in Ephesus were already scratching that itch. And Paul knows it will only get worse. That's exactly why Timothy can't afford to go quiet.

"As for you," Paul writes (and this is the fourth time in the letter he uses this phrase to set Timothy apart from the crowd), "always be sober-minded, endure suffering, do the work of an evangelist, fulfill your ministry." Four commands. Stay clear-headed. Accept hardship. Share the gospel. Finish what you started. Don't let the world's appetite for comfortable lies make you lose your nerve about uncomfortable truth.

I HAVE FOUGHT THE GOOD FIGHT

Now comes the passage that has echoed through twenty centuries of Christian history. Paul shifts from commanding Timothy to reflecting on his own life, and the result is one of the most moving paragraphs ever written.

"For I am already being poured out as a drink offering, and the time of my departure has come." A drink offering was a sacrifice poured out on the altar in worship. Paul sees his approaching death not as a tragedy but as an act of worship, a final offering to the God he has served since the day Jesus knocked him off his horse on the road to Damascus. And "departure" was a word used for a ship untying its ropes and setting sail. Paul is about to leave this harbor for another shore.

Then the three statements that define a life:

"I have fought the good fight. I have finished the race. I have kept the faith." No regrets. No unfinished business. No wavering at the end. After thirty years of preaching, traveling, being beaten, stoned, shipwrecked, imprisoned, and abandoned, Paul can look back and say: I did what I was called to do. The fight was real, and I didn't run from it. The race was long, and I crossed the finish line. The faith was entrusted to me, and I guarded it.

"Henceforth there is laid up for me the crown of righteousness, which the Lord, the righteous judge, will award to me on that day, and not only to me but also to all who have loved his appearing."

The Roman emperor may condemn Paul. But the righteous Judge has a different verdict. On "that day," when Christ returns, Paul will receive the crown of righteousness. Not because he earned it by his works, but because he lived the kind of life that proves his faith was real: a life that loved and longed for Jesus' return.

And the crown isn't just for Paul. It's for "all who have loved his appearing." Every believer who has kept the faith, endured the suffering, and lived in eager anticipation of Christ's return will receive that same crown. Paul opens the promise to every generation.

LONELINESS AND LOYALTY

Paul now turns personal, and the picture is heartbreaking. "Do your best to come to me soon. For Demas, in love with this present world, has deserted me and gone to Thessalonica."

Demas. Once a trusted co-worker, mentioned alongside Luke in Paul's earlier letters. Now gone. He loved the present world more than the coming kingdom. He chose comfort over Christ. Of all the people who abandoned Paul, Demas seems to have hurt the most, because Demas didn't leave for a mission trip or because of illness. He left because the cost of following Jesus was higher than he was willing to pay.

Other companions have scattered too. Crescens went to Galatia. Titus went to Dalmatia. Tychicus was sent to Ephesus, probably carrying this very letter. "Luke alone is with me," Paul writes. The faithful doctor, the author of the Gospel that bears his name, stayed. When everyone else left, Luke remained.

Paul asks Timothy to bring Mark ("he is very useful to me for ministry"), to bring his cloak (the dungeon was cold), and especially to bring "the books, and above all the parchments." Even facing death, Paul wanted to read. He wanted God's word close to him. The scroll and the cloak: truth for the mind, warmth for the body.

He warns Timothy about Alexander the coppersmith, "who did me great harm." Alexander may have been the informer responsible for Paul's arrest. Paul doesn't seek revenge. He simply says, "The Lord will repay him according to his deeds."

THE LORD STOOD BY ME

Paul describes his first court hearing in Rome. "At my first defense no one came to stand by me, but all deserted me." Not a single Christian in Rome showed up to support Paul in court. He stood alone before the judges of the most powerful empire on earth.

But not truly alone. "The Lord stood by me and strengthened me, so that through me the message might be fully proclaimed and all the Gentiles might hear it."

Even at his trial, Paul preached. Standing in chains before Roman authorities, possibly before the emperor himself, Paul proclaimed the gospel in its fullness. His concern wasn't self-defense. It was the mission. If the Gentiles in that courtroom heard the good news, then the trial was worth it.

"So I was rescued from the lion's mouth." Whatever danger threatened him at that hearing, the Lord delivered him. And Paul's confidence extends beyond the courtroom: "The Lord will rescue me from every evil deed and bring me safely into his heavenly kingdom. To him be the glory forever and ever. Amen."

Nero might execute Paul's body. But the Lord would save

his soul. Paul's final doxology isn't a cry of desperation. It's a shout of victory.

THE LAST WORDS

Paul closes with greetings and a final plea: "Do your best to come before winter." Winter would close the Mediterranean shipping routes. If Timothy didn't leave soon, he might not arrive in time. The urgency is real. Paul wants to see his son in the faith one more time before the end.

"The Lord be with your spirit. Grace be with you all."

Those are the last recorded words of the apostle Paul. Grace. The word that defined his life, his theology, and his hope. Grace from the God who saved a blasphemer and made him an apostle. Grace for Timothy, who would carry the torch forward. Grace for the church, which would need it in every generation to come.

WHAT THIS MEANS FOR US

First, the word of God must be preached whether people want to hear it or not. Paul's charge to Timothy wasn't conditional. He didn't say "preach the word if people are receptive." He said "preach it in season and out of season." Popularity is never the measure of faithfulness. The truth doesn't stop being true just because people stop listening.

Second, a faithful life is the best farewell. Paul didn't leave behind a fortune or a monument. He left behind a fought fight, a finished race, and a kept faith. That's the kind of legacy that outlasts everything the world values. The question for each of us isn't "What will I accumulate?" but "What will I finish?"

Third, loneliness is part of the cost. Paul was abandoned by almost everyone. Even in ministry, even in faithfulness, you may find yourself standing alone. But Paul discovered what every faithful believer eventually discovers: the Lord stands with you when no one else will.

Fourth, the crown awaits everyone who loves his appearing. Paul's reward isn't reserved for apostles. It's for "all who have loved his appearing." If you live your life looking forward to the return of Jesus, holding on to faith through every storm, the righteous Judge has a crown with your name on it.

TALKING POINTS

1. **Paul says, "I have fought the good fight, I have finished the race, I have kept the faith."** If you were to look back on your life at the very end, what would you want to be able to say? What would it take to get there?
2. **Paul warns about people with "itching ears" who only want to hear what makes them comfortable.** Can you think of examples of this in today's world? How do you guard yourself against only listening to things you already agree with?
3. **Demas deserted Paul because he was "in love with this present world."** What do you think that means practically? What are the things in "this present world" that might tempt someone to walk away from their faith?
4. **Even facing death, Paul asked for his books and parchments.** What does this tell you about the importance of God's word in every season of life, including the hardest ones?

5. **Paul writes, "The Lord stood by me and strengthened me."** Have you ever experienced a time when you felt alone but sensed that God was with you? What did that look like?

Paul's voice falls silent. His race is run. But the gospel he guarded, the faith he kept, and the word he preached didn't die with him. They passed to Timothy. And from Timothy, they passed to faithful men and women in every generation since. The same gospel that sustained Paul in a Roman dungeon is now headed to an island in the Mediterranean, where a man named Titus has work to do.

Turn the page.

11

TROUBLE ON THE ISLAND

Indiana Jones and the Temple of Doom has Indy arriving in a remote Indian village after bailing out of a cargo plane over the Himalayas.. The place is desperate. The crops have failed. The sacred stone that protected the village has been stolen. Worst of all, the children have been kidnapped by a dark cult operating out of an ancient temple deep beneath a palace. The villagers look at this stranger who has literally fallen out of the sky and beg him: help us. Restore what has been taken. Save our children.

Indy doesn't know what he's walking into. The cult is powerful, deeply embedded, and ruthless. The palace above looks civilized on the surface, but underneath it there's slavery, deception, and cruelty. Indy has to go down into the darkness, confront the evil at its source, and bring back what was stolen.

When Paul wrote his letter to Titus, Titus was in a similar situation, minus the whip and the fedora. Paul had left him on the island of Crete with a job that sounded simple but was anything but: "Put what remained into order, and appoint elders in every town." The churches on Crete were young, disorganized, and under threat. False teachers had crept in and were "ruining whole households." The island's culture had a reputation so bad that one of its own poets had called Cretans "always liars, evil beasts, lazy gluttons." And Paul had dropped Titus right into the middle of it.

Titus didn't need a bullwhip. He needed something more powerful: sound doctrine, godly leaders, and the authority of an apostle behind him.

THE GOD WHO NEVER LIES

Paul opens the letter with one of the richest introductions in all his writings. He identifies himself as "a servant of God and an apostle of Jesus Christ." Then he describes the purpose of his ministry in language that sweeps from eternity past to eternity future.

Paul's apostleship exists to promote "the faith of God's elect and their knowledge of the truth, which accords with godliness." Faith and knowledge go together. You can't have genuine faith without knowing the truth about who God is and what he has done. And real knowledge of the truth always produces godliness, a life oriented around God rather than self.

Then Paul anchors everything in "the hope of eternal life, which God, who never lies, promised before the ages began."

That phrase, "God, who never lies," matters enormously in the context of this letter. Cretans were famous for lying. Their own poet had said so. But the God who sent Paul and Titus to Crete is the God who *cannot* lie. His character is the guarantee of every promise he makes. Before the world was created, before time itself existed, God promised eternal life to his people. And "at the proper time" he revealed that promise through the preaching of the gospel, which was entrusted to Paul "by the command of God our Savior."

Paul addresses the letter "to Titus, my true child in a common faith." Like Timothy, Titus was a spiritual son of Paul, probably converted through Paul's ministry. But unlike Timothy, Titus was a full Gentile, not half-Jewish. His very existence as a Christian leader was proof that the gospel was for everyone, Jew and Gentile alike. The faith they shared wasn't exclusive. It was common, open to all who believe.

WHY CRETE NEEDED ELDERS

Paul gets to the point quickly: "This is why I left you in Crete, so that you might put what remained into order, and appoint elders in every town as I directed you."

The churches in Crete were new. Paul and Titus had apparently done some initial work there, but there was still much "left unfinished." The most urgent piece of unfinished business was leadership. Without qualified elders in place, the churches would be vulnerable to false teaching, internal conflict, and moral drift. Paul's strategy for protecting and building up the church was always the same: find the right people and put them in charge.

Notice that Paul says "elders in every town," plural. The New Testament pattern is team leadership, not one-person rule. A group of elders working together provides accountability, balance, and a wider range of gifts than any single leader could offer.

WHAT AN ELDER LOOKS LIKE

Paul now lays out the qualifications for elders. If you've read chapter 3 of this book (on 1 Timothy 3), some of this will sound familiar. The lists overlap significantly, because the character God requires of leaders doesn't change based on location.

"An elder must be above reproach." That's the overarching standard. Everything that follows fills in what "above reproach" means in practice.

In his family life, the elder must be "the husband of one wife," faithful to his spouse, and his "children must be believers and not open to the charge of being wild or disobedient." As we saw with the overseer qualifications in 1 Timothy, the home is the proving ground for church leadership. If a man's own household is in chaos, he's not ready to lead God's household.

Paul then shifts to the title "overseer," confirming what the rest of the New Testament makes clear: "elder" and "overseer" are two names for the same role. The elder is called "God's steward," a powerful image. A steward doesn't own the household. He manages it on behalf of the owner. The church belongs to God, and the elder's job is to care for it the way God wants, not the way the elder prefers.

What follows is a list of character traits, five negative and six positive, that paint a vivid picture.

The elder must *not* be overbearing (pushy and arrogant), quick-tempered (easily angered), a drunkard, violent, or greedy for money. Each of these represents a form of self-indulgence, a failure to control your own appetites and impulses. If you can't govern yourself, you can't govern others.

On the positive side, the elder must be hospitable (welcoming strangers into his home), a lover of good (supporting anything that honors God), self-controlled, upright, holy, and disciplined. These are the marks of someone whose inner life has been transformed by the Spirit of God and whose outer life shows it.

Finally, and critically, the elder must "hold firm to the trustworthy word as taught, so that he may be able to give instruction in sound doctrine and also to rebuke those who contradict it." This is the one "professional" qualification on the list. Everything else is about character. This one is about competence. An elder must know the gospel well enough to teach it clearly and defend it against those who twist it. In a church like the ones on Crete, where false teachers were actively working to deceive people, this ability was not optional. It was survival.

THE PROBLEM ON CRETE

Paul now explains why good leaders are so desperately needed. "For there are many who are insubordinate, empty talkers and deceivers, especially those of the circumcision party. They must be silenced, since they are upsetting whole households by teaching for shameful gain what they ought not to teach."

The false teachers on Crete shared many characteristics with the ones in Ephesus. They were Jewish or influenced by Jewish traditions. They were obsessed with "myths and genealogies." They taught things that contradicted the apostolic gospel. And they were in it for the money, "teaching for shameful gain."

But there was something distinctive about the Cretan situation: the cultural environment was especially toxic. Paul quotes a Cretan poet (probably Epimenides, who lived around 600 BC) who had written about his own people: "Cretans are always liars, evil beasts, lazy gluttons."

That's a devastating assessment, and Paul adds: "This testimony is true." He isn't condemning every single Cretan (after all, the elders Titus was appointing *were* Cretan). But he is acknowledging that the culture in which these churches existed was hostile to truth, self-discipline, and godliness. The false teachers were thriving in a soil that was already fertile for deception.

Paul's instruction is direct: "Rebuke them sharply, so that they may be sound in the faith, not devoting themselves to Jewish myths and the commands of people who turn away from the truth." The goal of the rebuke isn't punishment. It's restoration. Paul wants these people to become healthy in their faith, to stop chasing myths and start holding to the truth.

TO THE PURE, ALL THINGS ARE PURE

Paul closes the chapter with a statement that cuts to the heart of the false teachers' error: "To the pure, all things are pure, but to the defiled and unbelieving, nothing is pure; both their minds and their consciences are defiled."

The false teachers apparently had strict rules about what you could eat, what you could touch, and what rituals you needed to perform to be spiritually "clean." They were focused on external purity, on following the right rules and avoiding the wrong foods. But Paul says real purity is internal. If your heart has been cleansed by God, then the world around you is clean too. God's creation is good, and a believer receives it with thanksgiving. But if your heart is corrupted by sin and unbelief, no amount of external rule-keeping will make you clean. You can wash the outside of the cup all day long, but if the inside is dirty, it doesn't matter.

The final verdict on the false teachers is devastating: "They profess to know God, but they deny him by their works. They are detestable, disobedient, and unfit for any good work."

Profession without practice is hypocrisy. You can claim to know God all you want, but if your life tells a different story, your claim means nothing. The false teachers talked a good game. They sounded impressive. But their actions told the truth about their hearts.

WHAT THIS MEANS FOR US

First, God's trustworthiness is the foundation of everything. God "never lies." In a world full of deception, spin, and half-truths, the God of the Bible is the one source you can trust without reservation. His promises are certain because his character is perfect. When everything else feels shaky, his word stands firm.

Second, the church needs qualified leaders in every generation. Paul's strategy for a struggling church wasn't a new program or a flashy event. It was leadership. Find people with godly character, solid doctrine, and proven faithfulness, and put them in positions of responsibility. That strategy hasn't changed.

Third, what you are at home matters more than what you are in public. Paul keeps coming back to the family as the test of leadership. Your marriage, your parenting, your daily conduct behind closed doors reveals who you really are. Character isn't what you display on stage. It's who you are when nobody's watching.

Fourth, real purity is an inside job. External rules and rituals can't make you clean. Only God can purify a heart. And when he does, the change shows up in your life—not in what foods you avoid, but in the love, honesty, and integrity you practice every day.

TALKING POINTS

1. **Paul says God "never lies."** Why is that such an important statement, especially in the context of writing to churches on an island famous for lying? How does God's truthfulness affect the way you read the rest of the Bible?

2. **The qualifications for elders are almost entirely about character, not skills.** If you were helping choose a leader for your church, what would you look for first? Why do you think character matters more than talent in church leadership?

3. **Paul quotes a Cretan poet who called his own people "liars, evil beasts, lazy gluttons."** How do you think the Cretan Christians felt reading that? What does it say about the power of the gospel that God was building churches in a place with that kind of reputation?

4. **Paul says, "To the pure, all things are pure."** What do you think this means practically? How is inner purity different from just following rules?

5. **The false teachers "profess to know God, but deny him by their works."** Can you think of ways people today might claim to follow God while their actions tell a different story? How can you make sure your own life matches what you say you believe?

Titus has his assignment: appoint good leaders and silence the bad teachers. But leadership is only part of the picture. Paul also has something to say about what everyday life should look like for every believer on Crete, from the oldest men to the youngest women, from free citizens to slaves. Sound doctrine isn't just something you believe. It's something you live.

Turn the page.

12

WHAT SOUND DOCTRINE LOOKS LIKE

Harriet Beecher Stowe's novel *Uncle Tom's Cabin* tells the story of Tom, an enslaved man whose faith in God never wavers, no matter how terrible his circumstances become. Tom is sold from one owner to another, separated from his family, beaten, and eventually killed. But through it all, his character remains constant. He is patient when others are cruel. He is generous when he has almost nothing to give. He is honest when dishonesty might have saved him trouble. He forgives people who don't deserve forgiveness.

What makes Tom's story so powerful isn't just his suffering. It's the way his faith shapes everything he does. His Christianity isn't something he puts on for Sunday mornings and takes off during the week. It soaks into every corner of his life: how he speaks, how he treats people, how he responds to injustice. And the people around him notice. Some are moved to change. Others are shamed by the contrast between his goodness and their cruelty. Tom's life becomes an argument for the gospel that nobody can refute, because the evidence is standing right in front of them.

That's exactly the picture Paul paints in Titus 2. Sound doctrine isn't just a list of beliefs you carry around in your head. It's a way of life that changes how you act, how you speak, and how you treat the people around you. And when you live it out, even in the hardest circumstances, it makes the gospel beautiful. Paul's phrase for this is striking: believers are to "adorn the doctrine of God our Savior." Like a jewel that makes a setting look more beautiful, a faithful life makes the gospel look more attractive to everyone who sees it.

BUT AS FOR YOU

Paul opens the chapter with the familiar contrast: "But as for you, teach what accords with sound doctrine." Unlike the false teachers on Crete (who "profess to know God, but deny him by their works"), Titus is to make sure that belief and behavior match. Sound doctrine is healthy doctrine, and healthy doctrine produces healthy lives.

What follows is a series of instructions for six different groups of people in the church. Paul works his way through older men, older women, younger women, younger men, Titus himself, and slaves, giving each group specific character traits to pursue. The instructions aren't random. They're tailored to the particular temptations and responsibilities each group faces.

And running through every one of them, like a thread stitching the whole chapter together, is one word: self-control.

OLDER MEN

"Older men are to be sober-minded, dignified, self-controlled, sound in faith, in love, and in steadfastness." Older men have had a lifetime to develop either wisdom or stubbornness. Paul calls them to be the kind of men whose years have produced maturity, not just gray hair. They should be clear-headed, worthy of respect, and masters of themselves. And they should be "sound" (that word again, meaning "healthy") in the three great Christian virtues: faith (trusting God), love (serving others), and steadfastness (enduring patiently while waiting for the hope of Christ's return).

OLDER WOMEN

"Older women likewise are to be reverent in behavior, not slanderers or slaves to much wine. They are to teach what is good." Paul calls the older women to live as if they were constantly in the presence of God, which of course they are. Two dangers are singled out: gossip and alcohol. Both were common problems in the ancient world (and aren't exactly rare today). But Paul doesn't just tell them what to avoid. He tells them what to do: "teach what is good." Older women are to become mentors, especially for the younger women in the church. Their years of experience, their hard-won wisdom, and their proven faithfulness make them uniquely qualified for this role.

YOUNGER WOMEN

The older women are to "train the younger women to love their husbands and children, to be self-controlled, pure, workers at home, kind, and submissive to their own husbands."

Paul isn't saying that a woman's only sphere is the home. He's saying that if she has a husband and children, those relationships are her first priority, not an afterthought. Loving your family well is the foundation on which everything else is built. And the list of qualities Paul names—self-control, purity, kindness—are virtues that make a person beautiful from the inside out, regardless of what the culture says beauty should look like.

Paul adds a purpose clause that reveals his deeper concern: "that the word of God may not be reviled." The way Christian women lived in Crete was being watched by outsiders. If Christian homes were falling apart, if wives were acting in ways that shamed their families, unbelievers would blame the gospel for the mess. But if Christian households were marked by love, kindness, and mutual respect, the gospel would be vindicated.

YOUNG MEN

"Likewise, urge the younger men to be self-controlled." That's the whole instruction. One quality: self-control. For a young man in the ancient world (and, honestly, for a young man in any world), this was the hardest virtue to develop. The culture assumed young men were slaves to their impulses. Paul says otherwise. Through the power of the Spirit, a young man can master his temper, his tongue, his ambitions, and his appetites. And that kind of self-mastery speaks louder than any sermon.

TITUS HIMSELF

Paul turns to Titus directly. "Show yourself in all respects to be a model of good works, and in your teaching show integrity, dignity, and sound speech that cannot be condemned, so that an opponent may be put to shame, having nothing evil to say about us."

Titus isn't just a messenger delivering instructions. He's a model. His life must match his teaching. His motives must be pure. His manner must be serious. And his words must be so solid and blameless that even his enemies can't find anything to criticize.

This is the power of a consistent life. When your words and your actions tell the same story, opponents have nothing to grab onto. They may dislike you. They may disagree with you. But they can't accuse you of hypocrisy, and that takes away their most effective weapon.

SLAVES

"Bondservants are to be submissive to their own masters in everything; they are to be well-pleasing, not argumentative, not pilfering, but showing all good faith, so that in every way they may adorn the doctrine of God our Savior."

This is where the chapter reaches its most radical moment. Slaves were at the bottom of the social ladder. They had no power, no status, and no voice. And yet Paul says that even they can "adorn the doctrine of God our Savior." The word "adorn" means to decorate or beautify. A slave who serves with honesty, faithfulness, and a good attitude makes the gospel look attractive. Their character becomes a living advertisement for the power of God to transform anyone, in any situation.

This doesn't mean Paul endorsed slavery. His letter to Philemon shows that he believed the gospel would ultimately break down the wall between slave and free. But in the meantime, he wanted every Christian, regardless of their circumstances, to know that their life mattered and that their conduct could advance the mission of God.

THE GRACE THAT TRAINS US

Now Paul reveals the engine that drives everything he's just said. "For the grace of God has appeared, bringing salvation for all people, training us to renounce ungodliness and worldly passions, and to live self-controlled, upright, and godly lives in the present age."

This is one of the most important theological statements in all of Paul's letters. Grace isn't just the door you walk through to enter the Christian life. Grace is the *teacher* that shapes how you live after you've walked through. God's grace "appeared" in the person of Jesus Christ, and that same grace is now actively "training" believers to say no to sin and yes to godliness.

Notice the two sides of the training. Negatively, grace teaches us to "renounce ungodliness and worldly passions." We learn to let go of the things that pull us away from God. Positively, grace teaches us to "live self-controlled, upright, and godly lives in the present age." We learn to embrace the character that reflects God's own nature.

This is revolutionary. The false teachers on Crete imposed external rules and rituals. Paul says transformation comes from the inside out, through grace. You don't become godly by following a stricter set of regulations. You become godly because God's grace gets inside you and changes what you want, what you love, and who you are.

THE BLESSED HOPE

Grace doesn't just look backward to what Christ has done. It looks forward to what Christ will do. "Waiting for our blessed hope, the appearing of the glory of our great God and Savior Jesus Christ."

Christians live between two "appearings." The first was when grace appeared in the incarnation of Jesus. The second will be when glory appears at his return. Right now, we live in the space between. We've experienced the grace. We're waiting for the glory. And in the meantime, we're being trained.

Paul calls this future event "the blessed hope," and he identifies Jesus with an astonishing title: "our great God and Savior." This is one of the clearest statements in the New Testament that Jesus Christ is God. Not just a good teacher. Not just a prophet. God.

WHO GAVE HIMSELF FOR US

Paul closes the theological section by explaining what this great God and Savior did: "He gave himself for us to redeem us from all lawlessness and to purify for himself a people for his own possession who are zealous for good works."

Two purposes: First, Jesus died to *redeem* us. The language echoes the exodus, when God rescued Israel from slavery in Egypt. Jesus has rescued us from slavery to sin and lawlessness. Second, Jesus died to *purify* us, to cleanse a people who belong to him and are eager to do good. This echoes God's promise in Ezekiel that he would cleanse his people and make them his own.

The people Jesus creates through his death and resurrection aren't passive. They're "zealous for good works." They don't do good reluctantly. They chase after it with passion. Grace doesn't produce lazy people. It produces people on fire to live for God and serve others.

Paul wraps up with a final charge to Titus: "Declare these

things; exhort and rebuke with all authority. Let no one disregard you."

WHAT THIS MEANS FOR US

First, what you believe should show up in how you live. Sound doctrine isn't just for the classroom. It's for the kitchen, the playground, the workplace, and the dinner table. If your faith doesn't change the way you treat people, something is wrong.

Second, every person can make the gospel beautiful. Older men, younger women, teenagers, even slaves with no freedom at all, can "adorn" the teaching of God. Your life is either an advertisement for the gospel or a contradiction of it. You get to choose which.

Third, grace is a teacher, not just a ticket. Some people think grace means God forgives you and then leaves you alone to figure out the rest. Paul says grace actively trains you, teaching you what to reject and what to pursue. If you're not growing, you may not be listening to the teacher.

Fourth, we live between two appearings. The first coming of Christ brought grace. The second coming will bring glory. In between, we wait with hope and live with purpose. Knowing that Jesus is coming back changes how you spend today.

TALKING POINTS

1. **Paul gives different instructions to different groups (older men, older women, younger women, young men, slaves).** Why do you think he tailors his instructions instead of giving one-size-fits-all advice? What instructions do you think he might give specifically to people your age?

2. **The word "self-control" appears in almost every group's instructions.** Why do you think self-control is so important to Paul? What areas of your life require the most self-control right now?

3. **Paul says grace "trains" us to live godly lives.** How is this different from just being given a list of rules to follow? What does it look like practically for grace to "teach" you something?

4. **Paul calls Jesus "our great God and Savior."** Why does it matter that Jesus is not just a good teacher or moral example, but actually God? How does his identity as God affect the way you respond to him?

5. **Paul says believers should be "zealous for good works."** What's the difference between doing good works because you have to and doing them because you want to? Where does the "zeal" for good works come from?

Titus has heard how every group in the church should live and why. But Paul has one more chapter of instruction, and it circles back to where the gospel always begins: not with what we do for God, but with what God has done for us. The final word is about mercy, not merit, and it will change how Titus sees everyone on the island.

Turn the page.

13

READY FOR EVERY GOOD WORK

The 1996 film *Fly Away Home* tells the true-inspired story of a thirteen-year-old girl named Amy who discovers a nest of orphaned Canada goose eggs after a construction crew destroys the wetland where their mother lived. Amy takes the eggs home, keeps them warm, and waits. When they hatch, the tiny goslings imprint on her. They think she's their mother. Wherever Amy goes, they follow.

But there's a problem. These geese have never seen another goose fly. They don't know how to migrate. When winter comes, if they can't fly south, they'll die. So Amy and her father come up with an extraordinary plan. They build a tiny ultralight aircraft, and Amy learns to fly it. Then, with the geese trailing behind her in formation, she leads them on a migration route from Ontario, Canada, all the way to a wildlife refuge in North Carolina. Hundreds of miles. Over mountains, fields, and cities. A girl in a flimsy aircraft, leading a flock of lost birds to safety.

The geese couldn't save themselves. They didn't know where to go. They didn't even know they were supposed to go.

But someone came to them, got down to their level, and led them home.

That's the gospel according to Titus 3. "When the goodness and loving kindness of God our Savior appeared, he saved us, not because of works done by us in righteousness, but according to his own mercy." We were lost. We didn't know the way. We couldn't get there on our own. But God came down, showed up in the person of Jesus Christ, and led us from death to life.

This final chapter of the letter to Titus is Paul's clearest, most concentrated summary of what salvation is, where it comes from, and what it produces. It begins with how Christians should live in the world, pivots to the most beautiful statement of grace in all three of these letters, and closes with practical instructions that tie together everything Paul has been teaching since the first page.

GOOD CITIZENS OF A GREATER KINGDOM

Paul opens with a reminder. "Remind them to be submissive to rulers and authorities, to be obedient, to be ready for every good work, to speak evil of no one, to avoid quarreling, to be gentle, and to show perfect courtesy toward all people."

The Christians on Crete lived under Roman rule on an island famous for rebellion and disorder. Paul doesn't tell them to protest, revolt, or withdraw from society. He tells them to be the best citizens anyone has ever seen. Submit to the government. Obey the law. Be ready to do good whenever the opportunity arises. Don't slander anyone. Don't pick fights. Be gentle. Show courtesy to everyone, not just to people who deserve it, not just to fellow believers, but to *all* people.

This is a picture of what a gospel-shaped life looks like when it steps outside the walls of the church and into the public square. Christians aren't called to build a fortress and hide inside it. They're called to live in the world as people whose transformed lives make others stop and wonder what's different about them.

But Paul knows this isn't natural. It wasn't natural for the Cretans, and it isn't natural for anyone. So he explains why.

REMEMBER WHAT YOU WERE

"For we ourselves were once foolish, disobedient, led astray, slaves to various passions and pleasures, passing our days in malice and envy, hated by others and hating one another."

Read that list slowly. Foolish. Disobedient. Led astray. Enslaved. Full of malice. Consumed by envy. Hated and hating.

Paul says "we," not "they." He includes himself. He includes Titus. He includes every believer who would ever read this letter. Before God's grace found us, this is what we all were. Not some of us. All of us. The only difference between a Christian and anyone else isn't that the Christian was born better. It's that the Christian has been rescued.

Paul paints this dark portrait for a specific reason. He wants the Cretan believers to remember where they came from so they'll never look down on the people around them. You can't be arrogant toward unbelievers when you remember that you used to be exactly like them. You can't write people off as hopeless when you remember that God didn't write you off. The memory of your own lostness is the foundation for gentleness and courtesy toward everyone.

THE GOSPEL IN A SINGLE SENTENCE

Then comes the turn. One of the greatest sentences Paul ever wrote. "But when the goodness and loving kindness of God our Savior appeared, he saved us, not because of works done by us in righteousness, but according to his own mercy, by the washing of regeneration and renewal of the Holy Spirit, whom he poured out on us richly through Jesus Christ our Savior, so that being justified by his grace we might become heirs according to the hope of eternal life."

That single sentence contains the entire gospel. Every essential ingredient of salvation is packed into these few lines. Let's walk through it.

The *source* of salvation is God himself. "The goodness and loving kindness of God our Savior appeared." Salvation didn't start with us reaching up to God. It started with God reaching down to us. His goodness, his loving kindness, his compassion for people who didn't deserve it: that's where the rescue began. And it "appeared," meaning it showed up in history, in a specific time and place, in the person of Jesus Christ.

The *ground* of salvation is mercy, not merit. "He saved us, not because of works done by us in righteousness, but according to his own mercy." This is the heart of the gospel and the death of all human pride. We didn't earn our rescue. We couldn't earn it. Every attempt to save ourselves through good behavior, religious performance, or moral effort falls short. God saved us because of who he is, not because of who we are.

The *means* of salvation is the Holy Spirit. "By the washing of regeneration and renewal of the Holy Spirit, whom he poured out on us richly through Jesus Christ our Savior." Salvation isn't just a legal transaction where God declares us forgiven and then leaves us unchanged. It's a rebirth. The Holy Spirit washes us clean, gives us a new start, and begins the process of making us into new people from the inside out. And God didn't give the Spirit sparingly. He "poured" him out "richly." Abundantly. Generously. The way you pour water on a garden you want to see flourish.

The *goal* of salvation is eternal life. "So that being justified by his grace we might become heirs according to the hope of eternal life." Justified means declared righteous, acquitted by the Judge of the universe. And because we've been justified, we've become heirs. An heir is someone who has been promised an inheritance. Our inheritance is eternal life, a future so bright and certain that Paul calls it "the hope" throughout this letter. God promised it before time began. He revealed it through the gospel. And he will deliver it when Christ returns.

All three persons of the Trinity are at work in this passage. God the Father initiated the plan out of his loving kindness and mercy. God the Son, Jesus Christ our Savior, accomplished it through his life, death, and resurrection. God the Holy Spirit applies it to our hearts through regeneration and renewal. Salvation is a Trinitarian project, planned by the Father, purchased by the Son, and powered by the Spirit.

Paul marks this passage with his seal of approval: "'The saying is trustworthy." This is the last of the "trustworthy sayings" in these three letters, and it may be the grandest of them all. Everything you need to know about salvation is here. It is true. It is reliable. It can be trusted with your life, because it comes from the God who never lies.

DEVOTED TO GOOD WORKS

Paul draws out the practical conclusion: "I want you to insist on these things, so that those who have believed in God may be careful to devote themselves to good works. These things are excellent and profitable for everyone."

The purpose of understanding salvation isn't to sit back and admire it like a painting in a museum. It's to be changed by it. People who have genuinely experienced God's grace become people who are devoted to good works. Not because good works earn salvation, but because good works are the evidence that salvation has taken root in your life.

Grace that doesn't produce good works isn't grace at all. It's a misunderstanding. Real grace, the kind Paul describes in verses 4–7, transforms you so thoroughly that you can't help but live differently. You were foolish; now you have wisdom. You were enslaved; now you are free. You were hating; now you are loving. And the world around you benefits.

Paul then warns Titus one final time to avoid the things that derail the mission. "Avoid foolish controversies, genealogies, dissensions, and quarrels about the law, for they are unprofitable and worthless." Good works are profitable. Pointless arguments are worthless. The false teachers loved to debate obscure details of the law and speculate about genealogies. Titus must refuse to play that game.

If someone in the church proves to be divisive, creating factions and stirring up trouble, Titus should warn them once, then warn them a second time. After that, "have nothing to do with him, knowing that such a person is warped and sinful; he is self-condemned." Paul isn't being harsh. He's being realistic.

After two clear warnings, a person who continues to divide the church has made their choice. The community's health matters more than one person's stubbornness.

GRACE BE WITH YOU ALL

Paul closes with personal instructions that feel like a father wrapping up a phone call with his son. Come meet me in Nicopolis for the winter, once Artemas or Tychicus arrives to take your place. Help Zenas the lawyer and Apollos with whatever they need for their journey. And one more time: "Let our people learn to devote themselves to good works, so as to help cases of urgent need, and not be unfruitful."

Good works. It's the drumbeat of the entire letter. Paul started with it (1:16—the false teachers are "unfit for any good work"), built toward it (2:14—Christ died to create "a people for his own possession who are zealous for good works"), and ends with it (3:14). The proof of the gospel isn't just what we say we believe. It's how we live.

"Grace be with you all." The last word in the letter to Titus is grace. The same grace that appeared in the person of Jesus. The same grace that saved us by mercy and not by works. The same grace that poured out the Holy Spirit and made us heirs of eternal life. Grace is where we started, and grace is where we end.

WHAT THIS MEANS FOR US

First, how you treat people outside the church matters. Paul's very first instruction in this chapter is about being good citizens: gentle, courteous, ready for every good work. The gospel doesn't just change how you act on Sunday morning.

It changes how you act at school, in the neighborhood, and online. The world is watching, and your conduct is either an advertisement for the gospel or a contradiction of it.

Second, remembering where you came from prevents arrogance. Paul says "we ourselves were once" foolish, enslaved, and hateful. If God's grace found you when you were at your worst, you have no right to look down on anyone else. The memory of your own rescue is the foundation for compassion toward everyone who hasn't been rescued yet.

Third, salvation is God's work from start to finish. He initiated it out of his own mercy. He accomplished it through Jesus Christ. He applied it through the Holy Spirit. He promised it before time began. You didn't earn it. You can't lose it by being too small or too broken. And you can't take credit for it. All you can do is receive it with gratitude and let it change you.

Fourth, grace always produces good works. Paul hammers this point throughout the entire letter. People who have genuinely experienced God's mercy don't sit still. They get up and serve. They meet urgent needs. They devote themselves to doing good. If your faith hasn't made you more generous, more active, and more eager to help, something has gotten stuck between what you believe and how you live.

TALKING POINTS

1. **Paul tells Titus to remind believers to be "gentle" and to show "perfect courtesy toward all people."** Why do you think courtesy and gentleness matter so much to Paul? What does it look like to show courtesy to someone you disagree with or someone who is unkind to you?

2. **Paul says, "We ourselves were once foolish, disobedient, led astray."** Why do you think he includes himself in that description? How does remembering your own failures change the way you treat other people?

3. **Paul writes that God saved us "not because of works done by us in righteousness, but according to his own mercy."** Why is it so important that salvation is based on God's mercy and not our performance? What happens when people start thinking they've earned God's favor?

4. **The word "good works" appears over and over in this letter.** What's the difference between doing good works to earn salvation and doing good works because you've already been saved? How can you tell which motivation is driving you?

5. **Paul closes the letter with the word "grace."** Why do you think that's a fitting final word for this letter and for all three of these letters? What has grace meant to you personally?

Three letters. Two young men. One aging apostle who knew his time was almost up.

Paul wrote to Timothy in Ephesus and to Titus on Crete because he understood something the church has been learning ever since: the gospel doesn't survive on its own. It has to be guarded, taught, lived, and handed on. It needs faithful people who will protect it from distortion, proclaim it with courage, and embody it with lives that make the watching world stop and pay attention.

These letters are practical. They talk about elders and deacons, about widows and slaves, about money and false teachers, about how to pray and when to rebuke. But underneath all the practical instruction, there's a single, unshakeable conviction: God our Savior has appeared. He has saved us. He has poured out his Spirit. He has made us his own. And one day, the same Jesus who came in grace will come again in glory.

Until that day, the assignment is the same one Paul gave Timothy, the same one he gave Titus, and the same one he gives to every generation that reads these words: guard the deposit. Fan the flame. Fight the good fight. Be ready for every good work. And never, never be ashamed of the gospel.

The letters are finished. But the work they call us to is just beginning.

www.ingramcontent.com/pod-product-compliance
Lightning Source LLC
Chambersburg PA
CBHW051509050726
47594CB00010B/4034

9781971767345